CAMBRIDGE LIBRARY COLLECTION

Books of enduring scholarly value

Spiritualism and Esoteric Knowledge

Magic, superstition, the occult sciences and esoteric knowledge appear regularly in the history of ideas alongside more established academic disciplines such as philosophy, natural history and theology. Particularly fascinating are periods of rapid scientific advances such as the Renaissance or the nineteenth century which also see a burgeoning of interest in the paranormal among the educated elite. This series provides primary texts and secondary sources for social historians and cultural anthropologists working in these areas, and all who wish for a wider understanding of the diverse intellectual and spiritual movements that formed a backdrop to the academic and political achievements of their day. It ranges from works on Babylonian and Jewish magic in the ancient world, through studies of sixteenth-century topics such as Cornelius Agrippa and the rapid spread of Rosicrucianism, to nineteenth-century publications by Sir Walter Scott and Sir Arthur Conan Doyle. Subjects include astrology, mesmerism, spiritualism, theosophy, clairvoyance, and ghost-seeing, as described both by their adherents and by sceptics.

Mesmerism, Spiritualism, &c.

William Carpenter (1813–1885) was a leading medical teacher and researcher in London. Although much of his work focused on physiology and the nervous system, he spent a considerable amount of time investigating questions surrounding the relationship between science and religion. He participated in many debates on this issue, and was a member of the prestigious Metaphysical Society, which explored scientific and religious connections. In *Mesmerism, Spiritualism, etc. Historically and Scientifically Considered,* two of his lectures published in 1877, Carpenter sets out to question on scientific grounds the many spiritualist beliefs that were gaining popularity throughout Britain. His work covers topics such as odylism, electro-biology, thought-reading and clairvoyance. He locates these practices in historical contexts that often stretch back to ancient times, and gives modern scientific explanations for certain phenomena, all with the aim of stifling what he called 'epidemic delusions'.

T0382632

Cambridge University Press has long been a pioneer in the reissuing of out-of-print titles from its own backlist, producing digital reprints of books that are still sought after by scholars and students but could not be reprinted economically using traditional technology. The Cambridge Library Collection extends this activity to a wider range of books which are still of importance to researchers and professionals, either for the source material they contain, or as landmarks in the history of their academic discipline.

Drawing from the world-renowned collections in the Cambridge University Library, and guided by the advice of experts in each subject area, Cambridge University Press is using state-of-the-art scanning machines in its own Printing House to capture the content of each book selected for inclusion. The files are processed to give a consistently clear, crisp image, and the books finished to the high quality standard for which the Press is recognised around the world. The latest print-on-demand technology ensures that the books will remain available indefinitely, and that orders for single or multiple copies can quickly be supplied.

The Cambridge Library Collection will bring back to life books of enduring scholarly value (including out-of-copyright works originally issued by other publishers) across a wide range of disciplines in the humanities and social sciences and in science and technology.

CAMBRIDGE LIBRARY COLLECTION

Books of enduring scholarly value

History

The books reissued in this series include accounts of historical events and movements by eye-witnesses and contemporaries, as well as landmark studies that assembled significant source materials or developed new historiographical methods. The series includes work in social, political and military history on a wide range of periods and regions, giving modern scholars ready access to influential publications of the past.

Parliament and the Army 1642-1904

J. S. Omond's study of 1933 documents the historically problematic relationship between Parliament and the Army. Providing an overview of the 260 years which elapsed from the outbreak of the English Civil War in 1642 until the establishment of the Army Council in 1904, the book describes the phases through which the problem of political control of the army has passed. Omond draws upon a wide variety of historical material including biographies, memoirs, letters, parliamentary debates and newspaper articles in addressing how and why this relationship has remained of principal concern since the reign of Charles I. An Epilogue takes account of events from 1904 to the book's publication in 1933, and a chronological table summarises the key historical and political events.

Cambridge University Press has long been a pioneer in the reissuing of out-of-print titles from its own backlist, producing digital reprints of books that are still sought after by scholars and students but could not be reprinted economically using traditional technology. The Cambridge Library Collection extends this activity to a wider range of books which are still of importance to researchers and professionals, either for the source material they contain, or as landmarks in the history of their academic discipline.

Drawing from the world-renowned collections in the Cambridge University Library, and guided by the advice of experts in each subject area, Cambridge University Press is using state-of-the-art scanning machines in its own Printing House to capture the content of each book selected for inclusion. The files are processed to give a consistently clear, crisp image, and the books finished to the high quality standard for which the Press is recognised around the world. The latest print-on-demand technology ensures that the books will remain available indefinitely, and that orders for single or multiple copies can quickly be supplied.

The Cambridge Library Collection will bring back to life books of enduring scholarly value across a wide range of disciplines in the humanities and social sciences and in science and technology.

Parliament and the Army 1642-1904

John Stuart Omond

CAMBRIDGE
UNIVERSITY PRESS

CAMBRIDGE UNIVERSITY PRESS

Cambridge New York Melbourne Madrid Cape Town Singapore São Paolo Delhi

Published in the United States of America by Cambridge University Press, New York

www.cambridge.org
Information on this title: www.cambridge.org/9781108005142

© In this compilation Cambridge University Press 2009

This edition first published 1933
This digitally printed version 2009

ISBN 978-1-108-00514-2

PARLIAMENT AND THE ARMY

LONDON
Cambridge University Press
FETTER LANE

NEW YORK · TORONTO
BOMBAY · CALCUTTA · MADRAS
Macmillan

TOKYO
Maruzen Company Ltd

PARLIAMENT AND THE ARMY

1642—1904

by

LIEUT.-COLONEL J. S. OMOND

M.B.E., M.C.

Royal Army Ordnance Corps

"It is no easy matter to reconcile the institution of a standing
army with the genius of parliamentary and popular government, and the work was not done in a day."
Trevelyan, *England under Queen Anne*, I, chap. x.

CAMBRIDGE

AT THE UNIVERSITY PRESS

1933

To

W. E. C. O.

CONTENTS

Chapter V *page* 125

"Six years of peace"; localisation scheme; the Commander-in-
Chief and Childers; Commissariat, Ordnance and Pay under the
Commander-in-Chief; Orders-in-Council of 1887 and 1888;
Hartington Commission; Liberal Cabinet's proposals; resignation
of the Commander-in-Chief; Wolseley appointed; Order-in-
Council of November, 1895; Clinton-Dawkins Committee;
Esher Committee; the Army Council

PREFACE

I N the winter of 1927–8, the late Professor Graham Wallas delivered a series of lectures on "Army Control" to the members of the Army Class then attending the London School of Economics. He remarked that this subject was of considerable interest but, as far as he knew, no one had published a study of it. He added that possibly someone in the Class might feel inspired to write such a book. This small volume is an attempt to carry out his suggestion, and the author hopes that it may be useful to students and others who are interested in the subject of the relations between Parliament and the Army.

Apart from Professor Graham Wallas' lectures, the materials from which the following pages have been compiled are to be found scattered in histories, biographies, memoirs, letters, debates in Parliament, newspaper articles, etc., covering the whole two hundred and sixty years which elapsed from the outbreak of the Civil War in 1642 until the establishment of the Army Council in 1904. My authorities are fully indicated in the footnotes.

Without Professor Graham Wallas' encouragement and advice, which only ceased a few months before his death, the book would never have been written.

My thanks are due to W. Y. Baldry, Esq., O.B.E., the Librarian of the War Office, for valuable criticism and advice.

J. S. O.

December 25th, 1932

ABBREVIATIONS USED IN REFERENCES

Cardwell at the War Office: Biddulph, *Lord Cardwell at the War Office*.
Clode: Clode, *Military Forces of the Crown*.
Disraeli's Life: Monypenny and Buckle, *Life of Lord Beaconsfield*.
Fortescue: Fortescue, *History of the British Army*.
Lecky: *History of England in the Eighteenth Century*.
Verner: Verner, *Military Life of the Duke of Cambridge*.
Wolseley's Life: Maurice and Arthur, *Life of Lord Wolseley*.

CHAPTER I

Armed forces; the problem in England; Charles I and the army; Petition of Right; control of the militia; coercion of Parliament; Monk and the Restoration; impeachment of Clarendon; unpopularity of the army; James II; camp at Hounslow

THE preservation of internal order and the prevention of foreign encroachment are among the principal duties of all governments. If these duties are to be carried out, if domestic peace and freedom from invasion are to be vouchsafed to a country, its government must be prepared to maintain an armed force of some sort. It must be ready to expend the lives of its citizens and its treasure in their fulfilment. The weapons which have been wielded from time immemorial in so doing have been the armed forces of the different nations of the world. The raising of armies in the past for aggression against foreign states has been an easy matter. The call to citizens to rally to the defence of the fatherland has met with patriotic response. The creation of armies in face of national peril has presented no difficulties to governments. The defenders of Thermopylae and the soldiers of the first republican armies of France are examples of the spirit which actuates nations in time of difficulty. It is easy for governments to control these armed forces in times of actual conflict, but the task of determining their position in relation to the rest of the State in times of peace has taxed the ingenuity of statesmen and philosophers to its utmost throughout the ages. Kings and emperors, writers and politicians, rulers and ruled, have all wrestled with the thorny problem of the relationship which should exist between the majority of the population of the State and a number of men who, by the nature of their calling, must lead, as Plato pointed out, a life somewhat apart from that of their fellow citizens.[1] It is a matter to which special consideration must be given at all times in view of the fact that two special characteristics clearly define the difference between them and the majority of the normal citizens. In the first place, this body of men is entirely dependent on the State for its creation and its upkeep. It is clothed and fed, comes and goes, at the bidding of the State. It is increased or diminished in size by the orders of the State which it exists to defend in time of trial. The second characteristic affords a still greater contrast. These men are armed. The rest of the citizens are not. It is this fact that renders their position in the State a matter of such gravity. Being armed, they represent a force which can coerce the rest of the community and can overthrow the unarmed or civil government of the country if they choose to use the weapons which that government has placed in their hands. Thus it comes about that armed forces are the offspring and ward of the State, to live or die at the wish of the State. At the same time, they may become its masters controlling the means of destroying the State to which they owe their being.

Ancient and modern history are not devoid of examples of the delicate position created in the State by the existence in its midst of this special body of men. Their peculiar situation is not without influence on their attitude to the State. A tendency to assume privileges denied to other citizens can be traced, while from time to time,

[1] *The Republic*, Book II.

the brute force possessed by armies has been used to subvert the existing order of government and to substitute and, possibly, to enforce a political system abhorrent to the wishes of the citizens. The Praetorian guards at Rome and the Janissaries at Constantinople made and unmade governments. The victorious Cromwellian army supported the introduction of a new constitutional system in this country. Napoleon III owed his accession to the throne, in part at least, to the goodwill of the army which failed in its allegiance to the then-established order of government in France.

Various solutions of the problem of the position which armed forces should occupy in the State have been adopted, but whether they are the final solutions or not, it is difficult to say with any certainty. Political science is ever-changing and ever-developing. The constitutions of to-day, the established order of generations, may be overwhelmed in some world-wide cataclysm to-morrow. The civil authority may be supreme at one moment and, at the next, the armed forces may assert themselves and seek to establish a form of government which may or may not be more fitted to the political genius of the country. But, in any case, some form of control of the armed forces is necessary whether the central government be in civilian or military hands.

In the following pages an attempt is made to describe the various phases through which the problem of the political control of the army in this country has passed from the middle of the seventeenth to the beginning of the present century. It was one of the principal questions in England during the reign of Charles I. It was a main factor in the dispute between King and Parliament. It

was a contributory cause of the breakdown of the Protectorate. It remained unsolved after the Restoration and
was one of the difficulties which had to be faced at the
Revolution of 1688. The following year witnessed the
establishment of a form of control which, if but a partial
settlement, reached at a time of great uncertainty, has
endured as the basis from which all subsequent developments have sprung. To make clear the gradual creation
of a political system combining military efficiency with
parliamentary control, it is necessary to review in broad
outline the situation as it existed during the sixty years
prior to the settlement effected when William III and
Mary came to the throne in 1689. The spirit in which the
question was discussed in those troubled years was un-
likely to lead to the solution of a highly controversial
problem. Men's minds were inflamed by passion. Their
judgments were warped by prejudice. Political intoler-
ance played a part in preventing the calm consideration
of a difficulty which in happier times might have been
debated in a less heated atmosphere.

The riddle which faced the statesmen of this country
in the days of Charles I, and for many succeeding years,
was that of adjusting the question of the maintenance of
an armed force in relation to the prerogative of the
Sovereign whilst upholding the long-established rights
of the subject in regard to taxation and personal freedom.
Some politicians then believed that a personal guard for
the Sovereign would develop into a standing army which
would misuse its powers in the same way as the Praetorian guards abused their privileged position in the
Roman Empire. With some reason they considered that
the army would be used against the liberties of the sub-

ject. The Sovereign was equally suspicious of the motives of the politicians, thinking that they wished to deprive him of his rights in order to establish parliamentary control over the Crown.

The measures to be adopted for the defence of the country were a cause of continuous disagreement between Sovereign and Parliament. Any attempt on the part of the King to establish a standing army was watched with jealousy and opposed in every way. Parliament considered that standing armies were characteristic of foreign states where the military situation was entirely different from that of Great Britain, whose shores were lapped by the waters of the ocean and whose natural defence was the navy. Great Britain had no land frontiers coterminous with those of foreign states and was free from the danger of sudden incursions by hostile neighbours. It was considered that, as a general rule, the navy, supported by the volunteer trained bands, provided adequate means for the defence of the country. Other armed forces should only be raised with a definite object in view, and once that object had been achieved, they should be disbanded. Parliament gave no thought to the provision of an army trained in peace which would be ready in the event of an outbreak of war. It regarded a standing army as a thing apart from the rest of the nation, created and controlled by the Sovereign, disciplined by him and obedient to his orders. It feared the establishment of military rule. It dreaded the idea of imposing taxes to pay for such an army. On the other hand, the tendency of the monarchy under Charles I, and his sons, Charles II and James II, was to provide itself with an army with which to enforce its views against those of the people as expressed, however imperfectly, through Parliament as the constitutional mouthpiece of the nation. The Commonwealth and Protectorate period was one of purely military autocracy in which the army openly used its strength to influence decisions on political questions of all sorts.

The quarrels of Charles I and his Parliament were closely connected with the control of the military forces. Parliament opposed his request for military and naval support for wars with France and Spain. In reply Charles endeavoured to impose taxes without the authority of Parliament. The Petition of Right, to which he had to give his assent, followed in 1628. Among other points, it dealt with the grievance of billeting. The return of the troops in 1627 from the unfortunate expedition to La Rochelle had given rise to many complaints in Devon and Cornwall on account of forced billeting. The inhabitants were compelled to take soldiers and sailors into their homes with but little prospect of receiving any payment in return. They were further provoked by the terrible condition of the men, who were diseased, undisciplined, largely unclothed and practically starving.[1] The Petition stated that

of late great companies of soldiers and mariners have been dispersed into divers counties of the realm and the inhabitants against their wills have been compelled to receive them into their houses...against the laws and custom of this realm.

It prayed that the King would remove the said soldiers and mariners "and that your people be not so burdened in time to come". As will be seen in due course, billeting

---

[1] Gibbs, *Romance of George Villiers*, p. 287.

remained a grievance for many years and was frequently discussed in Parliament, but it was long before sanction was given and money voted for the construction of barracks in which members of the military forces could be housed. The Petition also asked that the commission for proceeding by martial law be revoked and annulled and that no such commissions be issued in future. This request arose from the dislike of arbitrary proceedings under so-called martial law which was not subject to the procedure of the civil courts.[1]

As time went on, the relations between Charles I and Parliament became more embittered, and a quarrel arose over the question of the command of the army. It developed in November, 1641, in connection with the reconquest of Ireland. Parliament would not trust the King with control of the army because it feared the purpose for which he might employ it. He was suspected of wishing to use it to bring about the overthrow of the parliamentary constitution. In November of that year, Oliver Cromwell carried a motion that the two Houses should vote power to the Earl of Essex to command all the trained bands south of the Trent and that these powers should continue till Parliament take further order. In the following December, Haslerig introduced a militia bill giving supreme command of all trained bands in England to a general appointed by Parliament.[2] This proposal was one of the immediate causes of the civil war. It asked the King to agree to surrender the control of the militia. In June, 1642, one of the nineteen propositions laid before him at York was that he should hand over the custody of fortified

---

[1] Maitland, *Constitutional History*, p. 325.
[2] Firth, *Life of Oliver Cromwell*, p. 60.

places and the command of the militia to an officer chosen by Parliament. The King refused, and the First Civil War began when he raised his flag at Nottingham on August 22nd.

It is unnecessary to follow the fortunes of that inglorious struggle between the Royalists and Parliamentarians, the first phase of which only ended when the King was executed in January, 1649. The conclusion of the second phase was reached when Cromwell died some nine years later, and the Monarchy was restored. It is important, however, to note that the parliamentary party, no doubt unwittingly, began to sow the seed of future trouble for itself in relation to the army before the war was over. At one time it proposed that, with the exception of General Fairfax, no officer above the rank of colonel should be employed in the army. Another suggestion was that a large part of the army should transfer itself to Ireland while the remainder was to be disbanded, but no proposals were made to raise money to pay the soldiers who were to return to civil life. Such actions helped to make the army into a machine for forcing Parliament to make concessions. In other words, the army became a political body directed by its officers and the agents of the regiments. For instance, in November, 1648, the army in the south addressed a "Remonstrance" to Parliament against the negotiations then under discussion at Newport with Charles I. The army demanded a rupture and the punishment of the King. When Parliament continued the negotiations, the army resorted to force, and the King was seized and taken to Hurst Castle, in Hampshire. Parliament, ignoring this high-handed action, resolved to consider the King's answer as a basis for a settlement. The army's reply was the arrest and exclusion of members from the House of Commons by Colonel Pride and a body of musketeers. Again, in 1652, the army considered that domestic reforms ought to be continued and petitioned Parliament for a dissolution after certain changes in the electoral system had been made. Efforts to reach an understanding failed and, in the spring of 1653, Cromwell and his soldiers brought the Long Parliament to an end by turning out the members and removing the mace.

It is difficult to see what Parliament could do in opposition to thirty thousand armed men, however strong popular feeling might be against the members of a powerful military party who were determined to assert themselves as the actual rulers of the country. Parliament had no means of resisting the army, which was able to enforce its will even if it was clear that it was not in the best interests of the nation to agree to its proposals. The position was reached when it was true to say that Parliament was the "creature of the army", dependent for its existence on the goodwill of a military organisation, which expected a docile acquiescence in its demands and was not prepared to listen to the edicts of the politicians sitting within the precincts of Westminster Hall. The most that Parliament would do was to vote money for the army for a period of five years only, which was an indirect method of declaring its right to determine at some future date whether the army should continue to exist or not. Cromwell, as Lord Protector, disagreed with this plan as his wish was to make it impossible for money once voted for the army to be withdrawn. When Parliament suggested a reduction in the army rates of pay, it was threatened with military violence. The situation was filled with difficulty and, as a shrewd observer remarked,

indeed there began to arise various forms of jealousy between the army and the Parliament. The latter claimed superiority in respect of its being the Representative of the whole English people; the Army, on the other hand, protected by its General, enlarged upon the services it had rendered to the State, and upon the blood it had shed in many conflicts, nor would it allow the Parliament to introduce reforms to weaken its strength.[1]

Matters drifted on in an indeterminate manner until January, 1655, when Parliament was dissolved. In October of that year, the country was divided into twelve military districts, each under a Major-General, who was granted arbitrary powers with a military force of some thousand to fifteen hundred men at his disposal. The Major-Generals were placed in control of local affairs and made responsible for the enforcement of morals according to the puritan outlook on life. They were charged to put down any tendency to revolutionary movements. They were, in fact, military dictators endowed with powers which placed them above the law of the land. The scheme was unpopular with all classes of society and was withdrawn about twelve months later. Clarendon says that Cromwell

discerned by degrees that these new magistrates grew too much in love with their own power; and besides that they carried themselves like so many bassas with their bands of janizaries towards the people, and were extremely odious to them of all parties, they did really affect such an authority as might undermine his own greatness.[2]

[1] "A Venetian Ambassador to the Lord Protector", *Blackwood's Magazine*, May, 1930.
[2] Clarendon, *History of Rebellion in England*, Book xv, para. 25.

The death of Oliver Cromwell on September 3rd, 1658, removed the power which had controlled the destinies of England, both at home and abroad, during a critical period of her history. He had governed the country by his reliance on the army ever since the battle of Worcester seven years before. The country was tired of military rule, and a gradual desire for the re-establishment of the monarchy was growing up. Richard, his son, who succeeded him as Lord Protector, had not the force of character, nor probably the ability, to cope with the situation which developed with great rapidity in the course of the next twelve months. A new Parliament met at the beginning of 1659, and the members supported him hoping that he would be less dependent on the army, less amenable to its wishes, more inclined to listen to their counsels, and less easily swayed by the fear of military violence. However, as Whitelock records, "the soldiers began to speak high and threatening".[1] A quarrel between Richard and the army soon arose over a request from the officers that Fleetwood, who was his brother-in-law, should be their commander and independent of the authority of the Protector. Fleetwood was nominated as commander, but Richard insisted that he must act as Lieutenant-General under the Protector. Parliament supported him in this view as a means of upholding the control of the army by the civil authority. In April, the soldiers forced him to dissolve Parliament. His resignation followed on May 25th, and the Protectorate was at an end.

The military party next attempted to govern by themselves. The first step taken before Richard Cromwell's

1 Whitelock, *Memorials of the English Affairs*, IV, p. 342.

resignation was to restore the remains or Rump of the Long Parliament which Oliver Cromwell had thrown out in 1653, but it was found that this remnant of a Parliament was most tenacious of its rights. The members told the officers "that the Parliament expected faithfulness and obedience to the Parliament and Commonwealth". Before anything could be done to settle the points in dispute, a rising in favour of Charles, the eldest son of the late King, took place in Cheshire. Lambert suppressed this outbreak. On his return to London, Parliament refused to agree to the conditions proposed by the officers, and members were prevented by troops from entering the House. The attitude assumed by the army in these disputes was that violence to Parliament might be used if the army considered that Parliament was in the wrong, "which gives the army a superior authority, and an inspection into the proceeding of Parliament".[1] The army had come to despise civilians because they were civilians. It endeavoured to govern without any civil authority. Taxes were only collected with difficulty. Quarrels divided the army, and the attempt at military government was a complete failure. The Rump was recalled for the second time in December and resumed its sittings.

Meanwhile, north of the Tweed, the army was not so violently affected by political considerations as the troops nearer to London and had taken no part in the setting-up and knocking-down of Parliaments. It was commanded by General George Monk, who had fought with Cromwell at Dunbar in 1650 and had been left in command in Scotland at the time of the battle of Worcester. After a period of service at sea, Monk had returned to Scotland

[1] Burnet, *History of his own Time*, 3rd ed. II, p. 63.

and reduced that country to submission. By 1658, Cromwell was uncertain of Monk's real attitude to the Protectorate, and the Commander-in-Chief in Scotland became "the object of all conjectures". When Richard Cromwell succeeded his father, Monk recommended a reduction of the army and the assembly of both Houses of Parliament. When, in October, 1659, Lambert and his supporters established a Committee of Safety, with Fleetwood at its head, Monk is reported to have said to his troops:

> The army in England has broken up the Parliament. Incapable of rest, it is determined to invade all authority, and will not suffer the nation to arrive at a lasting settlement.... I think it is the duty of my place to keep the military power in obedience to the civil. It is the duty of us all to defend the Parliament from which you receive your pay and commission.[1]

Monk's army was primarily a military force and everybody who disagreed with him had been gradually removed from its ranks.

After a period of delay while the situation in England was developing, he crossed the Border with some seven thousand men on January 1st, 1660, and reached London about a month later. The Rump was still sitting and wished him to coerce the City of London, which had refused to pay any taxes as it was without representation in that Parliament. Monk, however, forming the opinion that the Rump was detested on all sides, declared himself in favour of a freely elected Parliament. A dissolution was voted, and the newly elected House of Commons was filled with supporters of the Stuarts and a Monarchy. It

---

[1] Guizot, *Memoirs of George Monk, Duke of Albemarle* (Stuart-Wortley's translation), pp. 124-5.

was the natural turn of the tide. Men of all classes were weary of rule by army methods, and looked to the restoration of the old system as a means of escape from the tyranny of a military autocracy and from the recent forms of civil government which had proved to be but useless experiments.

In response to an invitation to return to this country as King, Charles, who was then resident in Holland, issued the Declaration of Breda, where Monk had gallantly led a storming party of Goring's regiment some twenty-three years earlier when he was a soldier of fortune on the continent. Amongst other undertakings, Charles offered to satisfy the army in regard to arrears of pay. The Declaration was accepted by both Houses of Parliament, and on May 29th, Charles entered London amidst the plaudits of a rejoicing population. The re-establishment of government by King, Lords and Commons was due to a large extent to the deep-seated popular fear of, and objection to, military rule, aided by acute divisions in the counsels of the military hierarchy. By the conciliatory terms of the Declaration, the new King had expressed his intention of governing with the aid of Parliament and not against its wishes as his father had claimed the right to do. Nevertheless, as matters developed, it seemed as if he desired to secure his throne by the retention of a strong, permanent force. It was not surprising, perhaps, that he should wish to do so. His father had failed to appreciate the parliamentary point of view. Charles II may well have thought that if he could control an army, he would ensure his own safety. Moreover, his life had been largely spent in France where the King was absolute and had well-organised and powerful military forces at his beck and call. Doubtless,

Charles had absorbed ideas about the kingly office which consorted badly with the views held in this country, even by those who had been most responsible for his restoration to the throne of England.

When he became King, the New Model Army of the Civil War was still in existence. Parliament's wish was to disband that army and to trust to the militia, which was administered by the Secretary of State with the local assistance of the Lords-Lieutenant, who enjoyed the patronage of the force. Its officers were country gentlemen. Its members were the non-martial, peace-loving inhabitants of the urban and rural districts. Parliament's distrust of the army was profound. It still feared that it might be used as a weapon for the coercion of the country. It was loath to give to the King the control of a force which would look to him for its pay and privileges. It was jealous of the army commanded, as it would be, by the King. Parliament distrusted the army and believed in the militia.

Whatever Charles' original intentions may have been, he was wise enough to accept and act upon the advice tendered to him by Edward Hyde, afterward first Earl of Clarendon. It was agreed that the army raised by Parliament was to be dissolved by acts of Parliament, money being raised to pay off the troops. But, whatever Parliament's aversion to a standing army may have been, disturbances in London, the threat of trouble in Scotland, and the necessity of throwing a garrison into Tangiers, prevented the total disbandment of all the then existing regiments. The King was allowed to keep garrisons in certain fortified places and to retain some of the regiments which had helped the cause of the Restoration. He seized the opportunity which these difficulties afforded, and raised the strength of the troops before long to some five thousand men. This body was the nucleus of an army which was further increased to a strength of sixteen thousand by the end of his reign. Thus, soon after his accession, he aroused suspicions of his ultimate intentions, especially as his personal revenue was insufficient to pay for such a number of men unless he was prepared to adopt measures which would bring him into conflict with Parliament.

The free Parliament, in favour of which Monk had declared, was dissolved at the end of 1660. It was succeeded by the so-called Cavalier Parliament in which the vast majority of the members were supporters of the one party with any decided opinions. At this juncture, this party adhered to the monarchy. Parliament met early in May of the following year and gave evidence of its strong bias in favour of the Royalist cause by restoring some prerogatives to the Crown. It voted that there was no legislative power in the Houses of Parliament without the King. It also declared that the

sole supreme government of the militia and of all the forces by sea and land is, and by the laws of England ever was, the undoubted right of the king and his predecessors, and that neither house of parliament could pretend to the same.[1]

As has been seen, the question of the control of the militia had been one of the causes of the dispute between Charles I and Parliament, and at the time of the Restoration, a bill was introduced to deal with its future organisation and administration. This bill was dropped on account of the strong opposition to it on the ground

[1] 13 Car. II, c. 6.

that martial law was provided in it.[1] The question was again considered by the Cavalier Parliament, and an act was passed permitting for one year the training of the militia and land forces under the Lieutenants to whom Charles had issued commissions. But it was not until 1663 that the militia was organised, and the trained bands, except in the City of London, brought to an end. The result of the reorganisation was to establish the militia with the approval of Parliament. The chief power over the force was placed in the hands of the Lords-Lieutenant who organised the regiments and appointed the officers. It was a local force. Punishment was meted out to the soldier by the civil authorities, and martial law was unknown to it. The militia thus became a constitutional force. It was felt that the nation had got something to counterbalance the standing army, which was solely the instrument of the Sovereign. It may be added that the militia was not organised in Ireland till 1715, while in Scotland it was not reorganised under Acts of Parliament of Great Britain until 1797 although Corps of Fencibles were raised before that date in the northern part of the kingdom.

In 1662, Charles married Catherine of Braganza. This Portuguese princess brought in her dowry Tangiers and Bombay, the first foothold in India obtained by the Crown. The possession of Tangiers necessitated a garrison for its defence, and a regiment of dragoons and two of foot were raised for this purpose, an increase in the establishment of the army which was retained by Charles after Tangiers had been abandoned in 1684. About the same time, Dunkirk, which had been occupied by Cromwell's troops in 1658 during the alliance with France in

---

[1] *Commons' Journal*; Cobbett, *Parl. Hist.* IV, p. 145.

the war against Spain, was sold by the King to Louis XIV for £200,000. This action was very unpopular in England, but it saved the King's purse £120,000 which he could spend on a further increase of his army if he so desired.

The war with Holland, when the Dutch fleet destroyed English men-of-war in the Medway and blockaded the Thames for some days so that London could get no coal, dismayed the country, and it was openly said that such things could not have happened had Oliver Cromwell been alive. The unwillingness to make even reasonable provision for the armed forces of the Crown was forgotten in this general censure of the country's unpreparedness for which both the Court and Parliament were to blame. The cost of the war bore heavily on the slender financial resources of the Exchequer, and a peace with Holland was negotiated at the first possible moment. The House of Commons had already set on foot an enquiry into the expenditure of the money it had voted for the prosecution of the war. It suspected that part of it had been dissipated on amusements at the Court, and it wished to assert its power in regard to the disbursement of public funds. In the days of the Long Parliament, it had been established that no taxes could be imposed without the consent of Parliament, and Parliament now began to question the right of the Crown to spend money without its approval. Clarendon foresaw that if this principle were once admitted, Parliament would be supreme, and a political system established which did not accord with his view of the best form of government for the country. His aim was the maintenance of a pleasant but impossible harmony between a King responsible to no one but himself, and a Parliament striving to control the whole range of public affairs. However, Charles, who owed his restoration to the throne more to Clarendon than to any other man, failed to support his minister when the House of Commons decided to impeach him on the grounds that

the Earl of Clarendon hath designed a standing army to be raised, and to govern the kingdom thereby; and advised the King to dissolve the present Parliament, to lay aside all thoughts of Parliament for the future, to govern by a Military Power, and to maintain the same at free quarters and contributions.

All that the King did was to advise his Minister to withdraw, and Clarendon retired to France, where he died at Rouen in 1674. From this time onwards until the end of the reign, Parliament made repeated attempts to obtain a reduction of the army, which was far too small to give the country any security in the event of its being involved in war with the powerful forces maintained by the King of France. It held that the alliance with France against the Dutch had been entered into "as an excuse for raising troops". It would vote no supplies. It argued that the army was a grievance, and that all troops raised since 1664 ought to be disbanded. It was felt that the King was inclined to depend on armed forces, which were a burden, and unlike the militia which gave "security at home for it would defend but never conquer us". It was said that

the keeping the Army up is certainly *in terrorem populi*, and the laws abhor all arms but legal arms,

or, again, to quote the opinion of a member of Parliament,

If any man is so hardy as to advise the King to govern by a standing army, he would subvert law, and it is against the government of the nation.

The exemption of the army under the Articles of War from the processes of the civil courts was unpopular, and billeting was once again a source of complaint. The use of the army for police purposes and the collection of customs as well as for suppression of conventicles, did not add to its popularity in the country.

In passing, it may be remarked that in Scotland the Convention of Estates was faced with a similar problem to the Parliament in England. The government's policy in the northern part of the kingdom was to turn the militia into a standing army. Five thousand foot and five hundred horse drawn from the militia were to be quartered at the expense of the heritors in all counties. Each soldier was to swear individually

to maintain the present government in Church and State, as it is now established by law, and to oppose the damnable principle of taking up arms against the King, or those commissionate by him.

By the time the Peace of Nimeguen was negotiated without Charles' knowledge between France, Holland and Spain in 1678, there were grave fears in England that the King would employ the army to make himself supreme. Evidence in support of this theory was forthcoming in a secret negotiation which Danby, then the Lord High Treasurer, was conducting with the French Court by which Charles was to receive a sum of money which would make him independent of Parliament. As soon as the House of Commons became aware of what was afoot, Danby was accused of high treason and impeached for attempting to subvert the government and to substitute a tyrannical form of rule, supported by a standing army, which had been raised for war against the King of France, but maintained after peace had been made, although an Act of Parliament had been passed for disbandment. The King dissolved Parliament in an effort to protect his minister, but the impeachment was revived in the new Parliament, and Danby was confined to the Tower of London. Requests for reductions in the army continued. There was also a demand about this time for the militia to be held in readiness because it was feared that there was a plot or plots to re-establish the Roman Catholic supremacy. James, the King's brother, was an avowed Catholic, and it was believed by many that the King himself was secretly a member of that Church. The Test Act had been passed in 1672 to exclude Catholics from holding any public office, but it was discovered that commissions in the army had been granted to them. Charles died before this question was settled.

His brother, James, who was fifty-two years of age when he succeeded to the throne in 1685, had taken part in four campaigns with Turenne and two with the Spaniards. He was interested in military affairs and had re-organised the Board of Ordnance on a system which was largely adopted in later days by the Duke of Wellington.[1] He had no confidence in the militia which was the only military force then recognised by law and wished to see it set aside. He desired to maintain and augment the regular army which had been strengthened in the preceding year by the arrival home of the garrison from Tangiers and of six regiments from Holland. The Duke of Monmouth's rebellion in the West of England and the

[1] Royal Warrant, dated July 25th, 1683; Stanhope, *Notes of Conversations with the Duke of Wellington*, p. 66.

attempted rising headed by the Duke of Argyll in Scotland no doubt emboldened him to approach Parliament with a request for assistance in the support of the increased standing army. His revenue was not large enough to meet the extra charges involved, and naval expenditure was absorbing considerable sums. The army was still regarded, more especially in the House of Commons, as a body associated with all the evils of the last half-century. It was thought to be an instrument of oppression. It was held up to obloquy as a weapon of the tyrant, whether he be King or Protector. The days of the Major-Generals were not forgotten. When Parliament met, opposition to the increases in the army was aroused by the King's request for means with which to meet the additional charges. It mattered not to the members that the King's supporters pointed out how incompetent the militia was, and how much superior a military force would be if it were a properly trained and disciplined body of men. The members of the House of Commons preferred to rely on a hastily enrolled militia rather than on a standing army, the mere thought of which filled them with consternation and alarm. They protested against the continual employment of officers who had not subscribed to the conditions imposed by the Test Act, even if the King declared that he could depend on those officers. James asked Parliament for £1,400,000. Parliament voted him £700,000, but for no specific purpose. The country was alarmed at his high-handed action in employing officers who did not subscribe to the rites of the Anglican Church. Protestant refugees who had fled from France after the Revocation of the Edict of Nantes by Louis XIV had spread tales of what might follow in the train of an army con-

trolled by Roman Catholics. The protests were not confined to the members of the House of Commons. Viscount
Mordaunt, afterwards third Earl of Peterborough, a man
who was to come to greater prominence during the war
of the Spanish Succession, said in a debate in the Upper
House that the evil which they were considering was
neither future nor uncertain. A standing army existed.
It was officered by Papists. They had no foreign enemy.
There was no rebellion in the land. For what then was
this force maintained except for the purpose of subverting
their laws and establishing that arbitrary power which
was so justly abhorred by Englishmen?[1] The King was
unmoved by the opinions expressed in either of the
Houses of Parliament and, refusing to part with the
officers concerned, prorogued Parliament the following
day. It was not summoned again during his reign.

From that time onwards, the sequence of events
marched rapidly towards the inevitable conclusion in a
country which was determined not to submit to an armed
tyranny. Some thirteen thousand to sixteen thousand
soldiers were quartered at the camp at Hounslow in the
hope that they would overawe London. Efforts made by
the King to get the officers and men to promise to secure
the repeal of the Test Act met with little or no support. In
Ireland, the King's Deputy, Tyrconnel, was allowed to
expel Protestant officers and men from the army to make
room for Roman Catholics, and no Protestants were
allowed to enlist. Desertions from the Hounslow camp
increased, and some deserters were hanged on a convic-
tion by a court packed by the King's orders. In fact, the
army was breaking in the King's hands, and there was

[1] Ballard, *The Great Earl of Peterborough*, p. 43.

no Mutiny Act in existence by which discipline could be enforced.

At last, the camp at Hounslow was given up, and the troops were dispersed to quarters in various parts of the country. They had given an unmistakable indication of their attitude to public events when they, in common with the sailors of the Fleet, had cheered on receipt of the news of the acquittal of the seven Bishops. The King had decided to reorganise his army, and had arranged for a number of battalions which had been raised in Ireland to be brought over to England. Irish recruits were sent to this country to fill up the vacancies in the English regiments.

It was these events, and certain other circumstances with which we are not concerned, that determined some of the Whig and Tory leaders to put themselves into communication on June 30th, the day after the acquittal of the Bishops, with William, Prince of Orange, inviting him to land with an armed force to defend the liberties of England. On October 16th, 1688, after making arrangements for the conduct of the affairs of Holland during his absence and fitting out the expedition, the Prince embarked at Helvoetsluis, but was driven back by contrary winds. He set sail again on November 1st. A following wind carried him further to the west than he intended to go, and he was pursued by the British fleet. The wind changed, drove the English ships back up the Channel, and enabled William to effect a successful and uninterrupted landing four days later at Torbay. After a fruitless attempt to oppose his army to that of the Prince of Orange, in the course of which he was deserted by a proportion of his troops, James II left England in December.

CHAPTER II

The army and the Revolution of 1689 ; Declaration of Right ; Mutiny Act ; growth of parliamentary control ; opposition to an army ; misuse of influence ; Militia Act of 1756 ; continuous neglect of the army ; the police

O N his arrival in London, the Prince of Orange summoned a Convention of the Estates of the Realm, at which, among other subjects, the future status of the army was discussed. Before recording the decisions which were reached on that question, it will be as well to notice certain steps that were taken in regard to the army during the interregnum between the disappearance of James and the accession of William and Mary. The army, like the navy, had played a somewhat ignominious part in the Revolution. The treatment it had received at the hands of King James had not been conducive to the establishment of a trustworthy force, and the weapon which he had attempted to forge for the government of the country failed at the critical moment. The author of *The Desertion* expressed the hope that

the flying of the brave army may be a lesson to *all* princes to trust more to the *hearts* of their people than to any forces without them. And if all this army could not or would not maintain him in his irregular way of government, what forces will be requisite to restore him against the three estates and the body of the nation ?[1]

Discipline had been weakened by the efforts made by King James to convert the army to his views on religious and political questions. On his departure, steps were

[1] *History of the Desertion*, vol. I, State Tracts, p. 94.

taken by the peers of the realm, who undertook to carry on the government of the country until some permanent solution of the crisis was reached, to recall the Protestant officers and men who had been disbanded, and to make arrangements for their pay and subsistence. Officers and men, who were Roman Catholics or of Irish extraction, were called upon to lay down their arms. The Irish troops were ordered to the Isle of Wight until transports could be provided to take them back to Ireland. It was recognised that a complete disbandment was impossible because James II was pressing Louis XIV to aid him to recover the throne he had lost, and the chances of avoiding a war with France seemed to be remote.

The problem of the army, with which the Convention was faced, was not simple enough to be settled by a series of executive acts. It was puzzling and intricate. Within living memory, the nation had had experience of military government. It had not forgotten the weakness of a system under which the army governed Parliament. It was now suffering from the effects of an even more recent attempt by the Crown to make the army its servant. An adjustment between these two extremes was essential. It required the introduction of a delicate compromise in the constitutional system of the country which would allow neither the Sovereign nor Parliament to claim and establish supremacy in the management and control of the army. The Convention met in January, 1689, and a committee, of which the chairman was Somers, drew up the Declaration of Right. It enumerated fourteen grievances, including the statement that "the raising or keeping a standing army within the kingdom in time of peace, unless it be with the consent of Parliament, is against the Law". At a later period, history was repeated when the Assembly of Massachusetts passed a resolution to the effect that the establishment of a standing army in the colony in time of peace was an invasion of natural rights and a violation of the constitution.[1] There were other important statements in the Bill of Rights, in which the terms of the Declaration of Right were afterwards enacted, but the salient feature, from an army point of view, was the foregoing declaration that the consent of Parliament was required if an army was to be maintained in this country.

The year 1689, in which a member of Parliament announced that he considered "redcoats" to be among "the curses of the nation", witnessed the passing into law of a measure of first-rate importance to the army and to its future relations with the civil authority. The circumstances are well known, but must be repeated here. A regiment was ordered to march to Harwich for embarkation for service in Holland. On reaching Ipswich, it mutinied and declared in favour of James II. It set out for the north but was overtaken at Sleaford, in Lincolnshire, by a force of Dutch cavalry, to whom it surrendered. Something had to be done to cope with such a situation, as it was obvious that William III could not depend on troops whose disposition was so uncertain. There was no Mutiny Act, and the existing law gave no powers to the Sovereign by which he could maintain authority over the army. The question was brought before the House of Commons and, as a result, the first Mutiny Act was passed. It declared that standing armies and courts-martial were unknown to English law, and enacted that no man

[1] Lecky, III, pp. 361–2.

mustered for the service of the Crown should desert the colours, nor mutiny against his commanding officer. The Act was only to be operative for a period of six months. It empowered the King to deal with military crimes which did not fall within the compass of the civil law. This Act placed the army on a constitutional basis and regulated the position of the Crown in regard to the raising and maintenance of a standing army. It stated in the terms of the Declaration of Right, that it was illegal to raise or keep such an army without the consent of Parliament, and declared that

whereas it is judged necessary by Their Majesties and this present Parliament that, during this time of danger, several of the forces which are now on foot should be continued, and others raised for the safety of the kingdom, for the common defence of the protestant religion, and for the reducing of Ireland.

Prior to the passage of this measure, military law had only been called into being in the event of war. As no army existed in peace, there was no need to have a special code of law with which to govern it. In the event of war, the Sovereign or the Commander-in-Chief issued articles of war for its government. Parliamentary jealousy of a standing army had always opposed the grant of any special powers to the Crown in case it should be interpreted as a recognition of the existence of the force. A new orientation was given to the policy of Parliament in relation to the army by the settlement made when William and Mary came to the throne, which approved the maintenance of an army provided the annual vote for men was passed by Parliament. The provision of means to uphold discipline, in the force so approved, followed as the next

logical step in the development of the constitutional relationship between the Crown, Parliament, and the army.
The declaration in the Bill of Rights, in regard to the
necessity of Parliament's concurrence in the maintenance
of a standing army, was repeated annually in the preamble
of the Mutiny Act up to the year 1878. Since that date,
it has been similarly inserted in the Annual Act, which
brings the Army Act into force. At first, the Mutiny Act
was considered to be a temporary measure, and it was
re-enacted for six months or a year. At one period, during
the reign of William and Mary, it was not in force for a
space of two years, and it was not until the reign of
George I that it was voted regularly. Its passage through
the Houses of Parliament was opposed whenever it was
introduced, though the volume of opposition gradually
diminished.[1] Its opponents argued that it was dangerous
to have one code of law for civilians and another for
soldiers; that it was wrong to authorise anyone but the
civil magistrates to suppress crime; and that it was unconstitutional to grant powers to the King to draw up
articles of war, a form of legislation over which Parliament exercised no control. Sir William Blackstone, the
lawyer whose well-known *Commentaries on the Laws of
England* began to appear in 1765, feared the danger of the
effect of the Mutiny Act on the liberty of the subject. He
held that the condition of the army was akin to servitude,
and that free nations should not allow the establishment
of slavery in their midst. No policy, he considered, could
be more foolish than to deprive of their liberties, the very

[1] A modern instance occurred in 1893 when the passage of the bill was
obstructed in the House of Commons: vide *Queen Victoria's Letters*, 1886–
1901, II, pp. 242–3.

people who might be called upon to defend those liberties.[1] However, it was slowly realised that no harm came
to the nation from entrusting the discipline of the army
to the Crown, and fewer amendments were made to the
Act as years passed. This growth of a more tolerant outlook was coincident with the gradual adoption of the view
that something more than a militia was required if England
was to pit her land forces against those of continental
powers. It was realised by degrees that it was useless to
send hastily enrolled troops to fight against the highly
trained soldiers of Louis XIV, for instance, and to improve
our army it was necessary to raise its standard of discipline
and training. This awakening to the real needs of the
situation mollified the attitude of the country to the
Mutiny Act. The settlement placed Parliament in an un-
assailable position, by asserting that it must sanction the
continued existence of the army every year by voting an
annual grant for its upkeep. If the reasons advanced in
support of the application for the grant were considered
unsatisfactory, Parliament could refuse supply, and the
army would come to an end automatically.

Moreover, the introduction of a vote for the army,
which was to be subjected to annual scrutiny, criticism,
and review by the House of Commons, linked to the
decision that every sum voted should be applied to the
service authorised by the vote, was another step in the
establishment of the future predominance of that House
in all financial questions. In 1665, at the time of the first
Dutch War, in the Parliament which met at Oxford, it
was suggested that borrowing on the credit of the vote
would be aided if the money were strictly appropriated for

[1] Blackstone, *Commentaries*, Book I, ch. xiii.

war services. Charles II agreed to the proposal, and a clause to give effect to it was inserted in the bill. This step still further strengthened the power of Parliament in matters of finance. The appropriation clause was inserted in all future money bills, although Charles thought that it was a sign of Parliament's distrust of his intentions. At that time, the usual practice was to vote the Sovereign the proceeds of certain taxes for life, which, it was estimated, would furnish sufficient revenue to meet the normal expenses of government. The distribution of the yield of the taxes was left to the Sovereign. There was no ministerial responsibility attached to the actual disbursement of the sums of money involved, which could be allotted as the Sovereign for the time being thought fit. In the event of war, the natural course was for him to come to Parliament, and to ask for an additional grant with which to meet the extraordinary expenditure arising out of the war.

In 1690, when supplies were voted for the war against France and in Ireland, Parliament definitely allocated the money to war purposes. It had already taken a step in this direction at the beginning of the new reign, when it granted a civil list to William and Mary, and voted a separate sum of money for the army. This system has been traced at earlier periods in our history, as, for example, when in 1348 the money voted was to be applied to the defence against the Scots, and again in 1377 when two treasurers of the parliamentary grant were appointed in Richard II's reign to receive and expend the money voted for the war.[1] But the appropriation clause of the modern type first appeared at the time of William and Mary. Since then, it has gradually developed into the system of

[1] Maitland, *Constitutional History*, pp. 183–4.

appropriation which is rigidly enforced at the present day. It means that Parliament expresses its approval of a certain service and votes a sum of money to pay for the due execution of that service, but the money so voted cannot be diverted from the service for which it was originally granted, and be spent on another service without the prior sanction of the Treasury. Thus, for instance, money cannot be diverted from some civil purpose to provide for an increase in the strength of the military forces unless such sanction has been obtained. Any surplus or unappropriated money, is returned to the Treasury at the end of the financial year and allocated to the reduction of the National Debt.[1]

The financial restraint thus introduced was, perhaps, the most powerful lever with which to control the Sovereign, that Parliament could have devised. It was a further development of the declaration that the maintenance of a standing army was illegal without the consent of Parliament. The confusion in public accounts at that time did not make its application easy, while the inaccuracy of the calculation of the yield of taxes, and the absence of any regular budgetary system, still further complicated matters.

Two further indications of the strengthening of parliamentary control may be noted here. The House of Commons began the system of appointing committees of their own members to frame and consider estimates and, where necessary, to review any proposals involving

[1] Although the present system began with the Revolution of 1688, it was not until the Exchequer and Audit Act was passed in 1866 that the House of Commons knew how the sums issued by the Exchequer had been expended by the Departments.

increased expenditure. At a later date, these duties became those of the Secretary-at-War, while the House of Commons only intervened on special occasions when they appointed audit commissioners with statutory powers. The modern system of audit has been gradually evolved, until there is an accounting officer appointed by the Treasury in each spending department. This officer is responsible to Parliament for the expenditure of his department being carried out in accordance with regulations. He has also to be ready to answer questions on the accounts of his department before a House of Commons Committee. At the War Office, the Permanent Under-Secretary of State is the accounting officer, with the staff of the financial branch at that office to assist him in watching the expenditure on the various votes. Another development in constitutional practice in regard to money matters arose in 1706, when many officers were submitting petitions direct to Parliament concerning their pay, which was in arrears. The House of Commons then laid down the rule "that they would receive no petition for any sum of money relating to public service, but what is recommended from the Crown". That is to say, it is a ministerial responsibility to introduce in the House of Commons all proposals involving the expenditure of public monies, and that no consideration will be given to it unless it is proposed by a member of the government. This system, which is still in force to-day, is unlike that followed in the United States, where any member of Congress can propose a grant or appropriation.

Parliament had thus established a standing army, and secured for itself certain rights in regard to it, which had hitherto been definitely considered as among the royal prerogatives or had occupied a vague and uncertain position between the Sovereign and Parliament. From this time onwards, the principal means of asserting Parliament's authority were based on the declared illegality of maintaining a standing army unless sanctioned by Parliament. The authority for its retention was renewed periodically, and was combined with the power of voting a definite number of men for a limited time with such financial supply as would enable that number of men, and no more, to be retained in military service for that time. This arrangement of the constitutional aspect of the question was probably the best that could be devised in the midst of the crisis with which the country was faced, and it still remains the keystone of the relationship between Parliament and the army. The settlement did not prevent many attempts being made to curtail the strength of the army. Parliament was not always persuaded by the partisan feelings of the opponents of the army, who still clung to the earlier faith of entire reliance on the navy and an untrained militia. Nevertheless, there was a powerful party of politicians in the country who conducted a campaign against the maintenance of the standing army and at times succeeded in effecting reductions in its strength. There was but little justification for their attitude in face of the military strength of France, which was then at the zenith of her power under Louis XIV. This policy can be traced through a long sequence of years. It came to the front whenever peace was made. No attention was paid to the wiser counsels which suggested that the lull in military operations was only temporary. The party hostile for the time being to the army, made an immediate demand for its reduction by the simple process of pro-

posing to curtail the vote for men. At one time, the
Whigs supported a large army, while the Tories clam-
oured for its diminution. Later on the rôles were re-
versed, and the Tories became the main supporters, and
the Whigs the chief critics of its size. Both parties in turn
overlooked the fact that no improvisation will produce an
army, unless there is a definite nucleus on which to build.

The administrative services of the army, so far as any
existed, were in a state of chaos, but Parliament paid little
or no attention to the subject. The campaign in Ireland,
where James II made an effort to re-establish the Stuart
dynasty, was carried on in face of deficiencies of all sorts
of stores and equipment which were required for the
well-being of the troops.[1] No serious effort was made by
Parliament to place matters on a satisfactory basis. It had
agreed to the establishment of a permanent military force,
but did nothing to ensure its efficiency. For many years
to come, Parliament was content to vote in a grudging
spirit the minimum possible number of men for the army,
and took no responsibility for any subsequent steps, which
were as necessary then as now if that army was to be
welded into a disciplined and homogeneous force.

It will not, perhaps, be out of place to refer here to
other matters which closely affected the army in its relations to the general public, and certainly had a bearing
on the feelings of the country towards the maintenance of
a standing army. As has already been seen, the uses to
which the troops were put at times, did not add to their
popularity. Extraneous duties, such as the collection of
customs duties and suppressing conventicles, augmented
the more purely political dislike which was reflected in

[1] Fortescue, I, pp. 343 *et seq.*

so many speeches and pamphlets. Billeting, however, was probably the greatest source of unpopularity. The civil population objected to being forced to provide billets. It had been a grievance during the reign of Charles I. It was declared illegal in 1679, and it was a matter of serious complaint against both Charles II and his brother, that they continued to resort to it as a means of maintaining troops without parliamentary sanction. Whether the troops were being illegally maintained or not, the fact remains that Parliament steadfastly refused to provide barracks, and the accommodation for the soldiers had to be found where it could. A change came over the situation when the retention of a standing army was approved, and billeting had to be legalised in the second Mutiny Act of 1689, the small existing barrack accommodation being insufficient for the number of men involved. Billeting, however, remained unpopular with the bulk of the people. It was hated by the innkeepers, who declared that the presence of soldiers at their hostelries drove away their ordinary customers. It is certain that it was a demoralising system from a military point of view as it involved the dispersal of the men in small numbers in bad quarters in every direction. The situation remained unchanged for many years because the political opponents of the standing army were always powerful enough to prevent the building of adequate quarters. They argued that their provision would facilitate the retention of an army, which was a menace to the constitution, though one writer, at least, acknowledged in 1723 that they would be "a vast ease to the inhabitants in most great towns".[1] Scotland was differently treated,

---

[1] Machy, *Journey through Scotland* (1723), pp. 24–5.

barracks being erected in certain places after 1715. The fact that billeting was not the regular practice in that country may have given rise to the well-known description in *The Antiquary* of the warm welcome given to the soldiers by Baillie Littlejohn and the other citizens of Fairport, when billeting parties arrived in that burgh. "Let us", said the worthy Baillie, "take the horses into our warehouses, and the men into our parlours—share our supper with the one, and our forage with the other." In Ireland, grants had been made for the erection of barracks in William III's reign. In England, the few buildings erected were put up in a grudging and parsimonious spirit. Sickness and a high death-rate developed among the soldiers in the garrison of Portsmouth, for instance, where the new accommodation built at the beginning of the eighteenth century was crowded to excess.[1] Towards the middle of the century, a change was gradually coming over the situation, to the regret of some of the politicians, who still disliked the idea of the standing army.[2] It was not, however, till 1792 that the building of barracks was taken in hand on a more adequate basis.

Opponents of the army also feared its interference at parliamentary elections. They considered that the electors could not exercise their rights in freedom if soldiers frequented the neighbourhood of the hustings. When the time came for the Convention of 1689 to be elected, William III gave orders that no soldier should appear in any town where an election was going on, so that the

[1] Clode, I, p. 222.
[2] See Lord Bath's pamphlet (1760) *Letter to Two Great Men* (Newcastle and Pitt), p. 35.

proceedings might be as free as possible.[1] This feeling of antagonism to the presence of soldiers at elections continued for many years. Greville, for instance, refers to the "discontent" of the populace, when a party of Horse Guards appeared at Covent Garden during the Westminster Election of 1818.[2] A soldier could attend to vote. It may be noted that a soldier was not admitted to the House of Commons until August, 1855, unless he was a member or had been called as a witness by the House. Soldiers were also excluded from towns during the sitting of the Assize Courts, in case there was any attempt to influence the course of justice. Until it was agreed to confine them to barracks while the Assizes were held, they had to be billeted in other towns and villages.

It is outside the scope of this book to attempt to describe either the fluctuations of the campaigns in which the army was engaged during the next seventy years, or the details of political affairs at home, while Sir Robert Walpole succeeded in maintaining the peace for twenty years. The disheartening defeats of Steinkirk and Landen, the glorious victories of Blenheim, Oudenarde, and Malplaquet, the Siege of Namur, immortalised in literature by the characters of Uncle Toby and Serjeant Trim, the rise of the great Duke of Marlborough, the political effects of the Treaties of Ryswick and Utrecht, belong rather to the general history of the times. The intrigues of the ministers, the influence exercised in turn by Sarah, Duchess of Marlborough, and her rival, Mrs Masham, over Queen Anne, the political union of England and Scotland, the accession of the Hanoverian kings to the

[1] Macaulay, *History of England*, ch. x.
[2] *Journal of the Reigns of George IV and William IV*, i, p. 4.

AFTER THE PEACE OF RYSWICK 39

throne, the two Jacobite risings, the loss of the American colonies, and the foundation of the Indian Empire, are some of the outstanding features of the political panorama of the first seventy years of the eighteenth century. While the army nobly played its part in these great events, it remained throughout the plaything of the politicians. If hostilities were imminent, Parliament would vote an increase in its strength. If peace were made, Parliament's earliest thought was to effect a reduction of its numbers. The opponents of the army said there was no need to maintain it. Any military support given to our allies should take the form of auxiliary troops, while the navy was increased. It was said that King William loved "a great army about him" so that he could govern "in an arbitrary way, as soon as he had prepared his soldiers to serve his ends". The Parliament of 1693 was called "The Officers' Parliament" because so many who held command in the army were then in Parliament, and it was given out that the country was to be governed by a standing army and a standing Parliament. In 1700 the Whigs, who had supported the King in his demands for increases in the army, were publicly characterised as "betrayers of their country, and as men that were trusting the King with an Army".[1]

The Peace of Ryswick was scarcely signed in 1697 before a controversy on this subject began between the King and Parliament. The Treasury was empty. The public accounts were worthless. The pay of both officers and men was seriously in arrears. An immediate reduction of the army was demanded in a flood of pamphlets, in one of which it was stated, that armies were "incon-

[1] Burnet, *History of his own Time*, III, pp. 116–17, 145, 352.

sistent with a free government, and absolutely destructive of the constitution of the English monarchy". In another pamphlet, published in Scotland, the author said,

Nor can the power of granting or refusing money, though vested in the subject, be a sufficient security for liberty, when a standing mercenary army is kept up in time of peace; for he that is armed is always master of him that is unarmed.[1]

The old argument that the fleet and militia were sufficient protection against attempted invasion was advanced again.[2] The only permissible permanent force was the King's Guard. The supporters of the army pointed out that our neighbours were armed, that France was very powerful, and that this country required a body of regular troops. A fleet might be wrecked and not be available at the critical moment. Somers entered into the controversy with a pamphlet known as his *Balancing Letter*. In it he advocated a small but temporary army voted annually by Parliament, while Defoe also defended its maintenance, in his *Argument Showing, that a Standing Army, with consent of Parliament, is not Inconsistent with a Free Government*.

King William, with his profound knowledge and insight into likely developments abroad, declared in his speech to Parliament, that England could not be safe without a land force. The ensuing debate showed that the long-standing objections to the army were still alive, and it was decided to reduce the army to ten thousand men. In the following year, the House of Commons made a further reduction which involved the disappearance of

[1] Fletcher of Saltoun, *A Discourse on Government with relation to Militias*, 1698.
[2] *Marchmont Papers*, II, p. 314.

the Dutch Guards and officers. The House of Lords acquiesced in this decision as it was useless for them to quarrel with the other House, in whose hands lay the power of voting the essential funds for the support of the army. It is small wonder that the King wrote to Hensius, the Grand Pensionary of Holland, saying that he was glad that "this miserable session of Parliament" was closed as it had despoiled the kingdom of its entire military strength. The futility of these proceedings appeared three years later when the strength of the army had to be increased again on the outbreak of the War of the Spanish Succession.

This lesson did not suffice to teach the politicians how much they lacked wisdom, for they proceeded to carry out a reduction on a large scale as soon as the Treaty of Utrecht was concluded in 1713. Two years later, they were faced with rebellion in Scotland, and with the necessity of again increasing the army. The Tory party, led by Harley and St John, had replaced the Whigs in office in 1710. They had long thought that their political opponents were attempting to saddle the country with a large, permanent military establishment, and produced a scheme to disband the regiments which were supposed to be partial to the Whig and Protestant interests. Their plan was to get rid of these units and officers, so that the path of advancement would be open to those who favoured Tory and Jacobite interests.[1] The situation changed again after the death of Queen Anne, when the King of Hanover came to the throne as George I. He was a Protestant, and the threat of the Jacobite invasion rallied the Whig party to his support, while the Tories were suspected of dealings with the Pretender. Tory

[1] Oliver, *The Endless Adventure*, 1710–27, pp. 157, 279.

officers were dismissed, and Whig officers recalled from half pay. New regiments of dragoons and of infantry were ordered to be raised, while the militia was embodied. One or two quotations will illustrate the weakness of the arguments employed by the opponents of a standing army about this time. Sir William Shippen, a leading Jacobite, in the course of a speech, in which certain passages led to his committal to the Tower, declared in the House of Commons that:

It would not be advisable for a Parliament, that intends to act rationally, and agreeably, either to the Principles on which His Majesty's Government, or its own power, is founded, to familiarise a Military Force to this Free Nation. For the very Name and Terror of it, would (without oppression) awe and subdue the Spirits of the People, extinguish their Love of Liberty, and beget a mean and abject acquiescence in Slavery.

Another member said:

I beg it may not be taken for granted, that, if we dismiss our soldiers, we shall therefore leave ourselves naked, and void of all Protection against any sudden danger, that may arise. No, Sir, Providence has given us the best Protection, if we do not foolishly throw away the Benefit of it. Our Situation, that is our natural Protection; Our Fleet is our Protection; and, if we could ever be so happy, as to see it rightly pursued, a good agreement betwixt the King and the People, uniting and acting together in one national interest, would be such a Protection, as none of our Enemies would ever hope to break through.[1]

In his pamphlet entitled, *Of Public Absurdities in England*, Dean Swift wrote:

A standing army in England, whether in time of Peace or War, is a direct absurdity. For, it is no part of our business to

[1] *Three Speeches against Continuing the Army*, etc., London, 1718.

be a warlike nation, otherwise than by our fleets. In foreign wars we have no concern, further than in conjunction with allies, whom we may either assist by sea, or by foreign troops paid with our money.

The opinion of those who opposed the maintenance of an army by this country was that our major effort should be made at sea, and not on land. They argued that there was no call for Great Britain to be involved in continental entanglements. They reasoned that the country's welfare was bound up with our trade, and that to embroil ourselves in war in Europe was to run contrary to the true interests of the nation. It was cheaper for us to fight at sea. Military as opposed to naval adventures would lead to increased taxation, and commerce would be hampered. The general lack of education, the absence of newspapers, the slowness of communications, and the insularity of a people cut off from the rest of Europe by the sea produced a natural desire to stand aloof as much as possible from quarrels in which the nation's interests were not clearly apparent. Members of the commercial community supported whichever party advocated the policy which they looked upon as most likely to bring profit to the country. The members of Parliament were for the most part ordinary people, and were chosen by a circumscribed electorate. The franchise was the privilege of the few, and not the perquisite of the multitude. Squire Western and the rest of his kind had never heard of the balance of power, nor of the dangers confronting this country, were the Low Countries to be permanently occupied by the power predominant for the time being in Europe. They preferred parliamentary representatives who would do what they could to maintain a policy of abstinence from active intervention on land and, in common with the commercial community, looked to the naval forces to secure further opportunities for the extension of trade in countries across the seas. They did not see that the growth of commerce entailed the expansion of the military forces, for trading communities required protection, which the army alone could supply.

During the twenty years of peace which began in 1720, the cry of "no standing army" was raised repeatedly. It was used as a weapon to ensure the defeat of a proposal originally made by Duncan Forbes in 1738, and approved by Walpole, to recruit national regiments in Scotland. It was not until 1756 that William Pitt, afterwards First Earl of Chatham, successfully carried out the suggestion.[1] Year after year, difficulties were made on points connected with the Mutiny Act. For instance, in the course of a debate on that subject in the House of Lords, Lord Wharton announced that, if during the King's absence in Hanover, the command of the army was delegated to one person, the liberty and property of the people would be endangered. On one occasion, a member of the House of Commons declared that "Martial law was growing upon us, would eat up the banks, and overflow the whole".[2] There were constant efforts to reduce the army below the eighteen thousand men, which Walpole considered to be the minimum possible strength in view of the uncertain political situation of the country at home and abroad. The factiousness of the opposition can be illustrated by pointing out that a considerable reduction was proposed by the

[1] *Culloden Papers*, p. xxxi. Lecky, I, p. 333 and II, p. 458: except 42nd (The Black Watch) which was regimented in 1739.
[2] Walpole, *George II*, III, p. 266.

opposition in 1738 at the very moment that they were urging Walpole to declare war on Spain. There might well be some truth in the story told of how Lord Granville, when asked by the King of Denmark about the bravado of the preamble of the Mutiny Bill, where eighteen thousand men were given as the strength of the army, answered, "One day can make these eighteen, fifty thousand".[1] So light-heartedly was the army question taken, that it was believed, no doubt, that thirty-two thousand recruits were soldiers, and fit to take the field, as soon as they were enlisted. The lack of responsibility was astonishing. In his earlier days, when he was Lord Carteret, Granville, in conjunction with Lord Chesterfield, declaimed against the maintenance of a standing army in peace when neither internal nor external dangers seemed to threaten the tranquillity of the country. The opponents of the army were unmoved by the wisdom of Lord Chancellor Hardwicke, who pointed out various dangers besetting the country, such as the possibility of a Jacobite rising, and the helplessness of the nation, if there were no military force with which to meet it.[2] Seven years later the folly of their attitude was revealed in all its nakedness, for the Rebellion of 1745 found this country practically without any regular army at home, and dependent on an unreliable, untrained, and almost unarmed militia.

At this period of history, political influence was fully used to help relatives and supporters of the government to promotion. Opposition to the wishes of the Court or the ministers was followed by disciplinary action. For example, Queen Anne instructed the Duke of Marl-

[1] Walpole, *George II*, 1, p. 253.
[2] Yorke, *Life of Lord Chancellor Hardwicke*, 1, pp. 184–5.

borough to give the command of a regiment to Colonel Hill, brother of her favourite, Mrs Masham, but withdrew her order, when threatened that Parliament would suspend the voting of supplies if she insisted on the Commander-in-Chief acquiescing in a step of which he did not approve. Later on, William Pitt lost his cornetcy in Lord Cobham's regiment for speaking in support of the opposition. Lord Cobham and the Duke of Bolton were both deprived of their commands for venturing to vote against Walpole's Excise Bill. Lord Stair had his regiment taken from him for supporting a bill of which George II did not approve. Lord Westmoreland ceased to be a captain in a troop of the Horse Guards for voting in opposition to the wishes of the Court in 1737. Lord Bristol, who was a strong opponent of the standing army, practically forced his grandson to resign his commission, by inserting a clause in his will which penalised his son's child because he was commissioned. Such actions, together with the granting of commissions to those who could command sufficient "senatorial influence" dragged what ought always to be a non-political organisation into a too close relationship with party politics. Lord Waldegrave, writing of the state of parties in 1754, says that Mr Fox had the support of the Duke of Cumberland, and the distribution of military preferment "which added greatly to his strength, by furnishing the means of gratifying his dependents".[1] Officers were either Hanoverian or Jacobite. Merit had little or no reward. The successful place-hunter was the successful officer. Nothing was done to improve the army, which was despised at the end of the long peace which Walpole strove so hard to maintain. It

[1] *Memoirs*, p. 21.

was not protected against the attacks of the party politicians, and when war broke out against France in May,
1756, it was still in a parlous state. It was insufficient to
ensure the defence of the country from invasion, and a
force of Hessian and Hanoverian soldiers had to be
brought over for this purpose. "What an inglorious
picture for this country", said Pitt, "to figure gentlemen
driven by an invasion like a flock of sheep, and forced to
send their money abroad to buy courage and defence!"[1]
It was a pitiable condition for the country, but the reason
is to be found in the years of neglect, and the chronic
jealousy felt by Parliament for the army. Proposals made
to reorganise the militia as a defence against invasion
were passed by the House of Commons, but were rejected by the House of Lords, where the Duke of Newcastle considered that the plan suggested would tend to
make the country a military country and government,
more than any scheme he had seen. He was convinced,
he wrote to Lord Hardwicke in 1760, that the establishment of the militia would be the ruin of the constitution
and the immediate destruction of the Whig party.[2] When
Pitt joined the Duke of Devonshire in the following year,
he made it a condition of his service in the ministry, that
some measure for the reform of the militia should be
undertaken. The Militia Act of 1757 was an attempt to
translate into fact the theory which had long been held by
Parliament, that it was possible to develop that force as a
substitute for the regular army. It was hoped that the
militia would not obey orders blindly, as the regular
soldiers did, and that it would prove to be a "good

[1] Walpole, *George II*, II, p. 101.
[2] Namier, *England in the Age of the American Revolution*, p. 134.

resource in case of general danger". No permanent
financial arrangements were made, an intentional omis-
sion necessitating a yearly act for pay and clothing. The
House of Commons thus secured control on the same
basis as it controlled the regular army. There were to be
only twenty-eight days' drill annually, in a period of
three years' service. The men were to be obtained by
ballot, and were to be Protestants by birth. The Act was
unpopular, and there were riots in different parts of the
country when it was put into force. The Tories, as the
opposition party, felt that they must be against it. As a
military force, the troops so raised were inefficient. Discipline was bad. Drill was inadequate. However, for the
next fifty years, Parliament was able to congratulate itself
on the existence of an army of some sort, which represented England in a way that no regular army could do,
with landowners as officers of "a respectable, military
force", as it was described in the preamble of the Militia
Act of 1786.

Throughout the middle of the eighteenth century,
British arms were successful in many campaigns despite
the failure of some of the minor expeditions which were
planned and supported by ministers. The battle of Plassey
secured Bengal for England. Quebec and Goree were
captured. The battle of Minden was won. Masulipatam
fell to English arms while the victory of Wandewash
saved Madras and broke the power of France in India.
Hawke and Boscawen gained successes at sea. Despite
these unparalleled exertions, which did so much towards
the foundation and expansion of the modern British Empire, the army remained an object of suspicion. People
disliked the soldiers. The old fear, that barracks would be

erected, still remained as alive as ever. No interest was taken in the efficiency of what Junius described as "a gallant army, which never fought unwillingly but against their fellow-subjects, mouldering away for want of the direction of a man of common abilities and spirit". The policy of keeping the number of soldiers at as low a level as possible, was based on a desire to reduce expenditure, and on the fear of military intervention in the civil government of the country. There were even complaints about the use of the army in London at the time of the Wilkes' riots, when there was no police force in existence, and the regiments employed had saved the metropolis from much suffering at the hands of the mob. George III, who considered that the army should be entirely in the hands of the Crown, encouraged the fears of the politicians. In the earlier part of his reign he saw that the soldiers were instructed to vote for the King's party. "I have", he wrote to Lord North in October, 1774, "apprised Lord Delawar to have the Horse and Grenadier Guards privately spoke to for their votes. They have a large number of votes." The practice of depriving officers of the command of their regiments was continued, because in certain circumstances they "dared to act with spirit and independence against the arbitrary measures of the Court".[1] This use of political pressure placed officers in a difficult position. They had either to approve of the practice, or to expose themselves to the resentment of the Crown, and of a set of ministers supported by it. One minister is reported to have said, "the King cannot trust his army in the hands of a man who votes in Parliament against him".[2] The last case occurred in 1764, when

---

[1] Walpole, *George III*, I, p. 337.　　[2] *Ibid.* p. 342.

General Henry Seymour Conway was dismissed for opposing the wishes of the Court. Since that date, commissions in both army and navy have been held without reference to political opinions.[1]

The expansion of the Empire, after the Treaty of Paris in 1763, did not arouse the politicians to the imperative necessity of keeping an army capable of defending the country's fresh commitments. They were too greatly occupied with the pleasant pastime of place-hunting and squabbling amongst themselves to undertake any survey of the situation at home and overseas. Even when the grave difficulties in the North American colonies were obviously leading to serious trouble, the ministers were unwilling to follow the advice of the King, who suggested an augmentation of both army and navy.[2] The regular army had to be assisted by the hiring of German mercenaries. A bill to authorise the embodiment of the militia in time of rebellion was opposed on the grounds that it would be granting a dangerous power to the Crown, and was alien to the constitutional theory of the militia as a local force for home defence. When George III, as Elector of Hanover, lent some two thousand Hanoverian troops to garrison Gibraltar and Minorca in 1776 so as to set free a corresponding number of British troops, motions were made in both Houses of Parliament to the effect that it was an unconstitutional action, and a violation of the Act of Settlement.[3] Permission to raise the militia in Scotland was refused. After the defeat at

[1] Anson, *Law and Custom of the Constitution*, II, Pt I, p. 125.
[2] Letter of 26th August, 1775, George III to Lord North, *Correspondence of George III and Lord North*, I, pp. 265–6.
[3] Lecky, IV, p. 440.

Saratoga, the opposition discouraged the raising of independent companies by private subscriptions on the grounds that it was unconstitutional and dangerous to liberty.[1] Proposals to fortify Plymouth and Portsmouth in 1786 were opposed by the old familiar argument that strong places would be used as instruments for the subversion of the liberties of the people by an ambitious and ill-advised King. Existing fortifications were stupidly described as "seminaries for Praetorian bands".[2] When, a few years later, it was proposed to enlist a number of French Royalists in the British army, Colonel Tarleton in opposing the bill in the House of Commons, contended that "the passing this bill will destroy the privileges of Magna Charta, undermine the Bill of Rights, and finally annihilate the British Constitution".[3]

After the recognition of the Independence of the United States of America in 1782, and the signature of the Treaty of Versailles in 1783, which marked the end o hostilities between this country, France and Spain, the political controversies about the army became of less immediate importance so far as the government and Parliament were concerned. The customary reduction of its strength was duly carried out, and interest in it and its affairs were lost. Its great services in the past were forgotten amid the welter of party politics. No effort was made to improve the lot of the soldier, and nothing was done to attract a better class of recruit to the colours. Ten years later, when the younger Pitt's dreams of peace were rudely shattered by the roar of the artillery of

[1] Lecky, IV, p. 440.
[2] *Parl. Hist.* XXVI, pp. 1097 *et seq.*
[3] *Ibid.* XXVI, p. 387.

revolutionary France, a British army was sent into the field without transport, without medical stores, and without reserves of ammunition.[1]

This new war, which began in 1793, came to a second temporary cessation when the Emperor Napoleon abdicated in 1814. By the subsequent first Peace of Paris, among other arrangements, it was agreed that a general congress of the European Powers should meet at Vienna in an endeavour to determine various details connected with the settlement of the future political arrangements of Europe. The Congress assembled in due course and was still sitting, when the dramatic news arrived that Napoleon had escaped from Elba and had landed in France on March 1st, 1815. The manner of his reception in that country made it manifest that he would be acclaimed as Emperor again, and the war-weary states of Europe turned from the pursuits of peace to preparations for war.

The Duke of Wellington was placed in command of the British army, which was ordered to assemble in Belgium. It was but a shadow of the old army, which he had led victoriously across the Pyrenees into France but a year before. A reduction of forty-seven thousand men had been made in the strength of the army by the end of 1814, despite the fact that there was then no certainty that peace was likely to be durable.[2] Ministers had been anxious to reduce expenditure as rapidly as possible, and had preferred the risks of a premature disbandment of the army to the odium of retaining it at war strength. The orders for the despatch of the forces to the Lowlands

---

[1] Fortescue, IV, Pt I, pp. 66, 95.
[2] *Ibid.* x, p. 228.

found the artillery short of drivers, the infantry under strength and untrained, and the cavalry only able to muster three instead of four squadrons.[1] The Hundred Days were followed by the second Treaty of Paris, which was signed in November, 1815. The peace of Europe was not disturbed again until the outbreak of the Crimean War in 1854, except by internal troubles in various continental countries. So far as the army in this country was concerned, the immediate consequence of the return of peace was to bring about a reduction in its strength in accordance with time-honoured custom. The old arguments that armies were only required for war, and that the sooner they were disbanded after peace had been made, the better it was for the nation, were advanced again. If war broke out afresh, there would be time to improvise a force to meet the new emergency. It was not surprising, perhaps, that there should have been a feeling of relief, a determination to put aside the panoply of war, after a period of twenty-two years during which there had been but two short periods of spasmodic and uneasy peace. The country was terribly impoverished. Taxation was high. Poverty and unemployment were rife, and the disbandment of the armed forces of the Crown added to the difficulties of the situation, as there was no chance of the men thus liberated from military service being absorbed at once in the industrial and commercial life of the country. Economy was essential if the country was to regain any measure of prosperity. It was fervently hoped that no cause existed for further wars. It was difficult to get money voted by Parliament for the army. The estimates were attacked, and particularly that for the staff.

[1] Fortescue, *Wellington*, pp. 169–70.

The volunteers disappeared, while the militia was not enrolled. The only reserve consisted of a number of pensioners. It was argued that small peace establishments were all that were necessary, and it was with difficulty that sanction was obtained for the retention of the exiguous numbers to which a hostile and indifferent Parliament agreed.[1] For many years but little time was spent in parliamentary discussions on questions of defence. The Secretary-at-War had few questions to answer. Joseph Hume, the leader of the Radicals and the economists, proposed reductions in the estimates, but his followers were only a handful. There were no important debates on army reorganisation such as marked the last thirty years of the nineteenth and the beginning of the present century. The lessons of the war were forgotten. The increase in colonial possessions and their defence, which was the responsibility of this country, were largely overlooked.[2] The Secretary of State for War and the Colonies, in common with the other ministers, were not unnaturally predisposed to devote more time and attention to colonial rather than to military matters.[3] In addition, the disturbed internal state of the country was a cause of much preoccupation to the Cabinet. Exception was taken to the number of officers and men who were to be seen in uniform in the streets of London. The reception, in certain circles, of a proposal to establish a club for naval and military officers, in which Thomas Graham, Lord Lynedoch, took a considerable part, is illustrative of the attitude

[1] Greville records in his *Journal*, i, p. 45, under April 19th, 1821, that when the Army Estimates came up for discussion in the House of Commons "almost all the members went away".

[2] *Parl. Debates*, xxxiii, pp. 998, 999, 1203.

[3] Anson, *Law and Custom of the Constitution*, ii, Pt i, p. 166.

adopted by some of the political leaders towards the army. Huskisson wrote to him expressing the fears entertained by the Prime Minister, Lord Liverpool, of the effect of the club's establishment on the "general feelings of Englishmen respecting military interference". Lord Liverpool considered it

a most ill-advised measure, and so far from being serviceable to the army, it will inevitably create a prejudice against that branch of our military establishment, and we shall feel the effects of it even in Parliament, when we consider the question of a peace establishment.

Lord St Vincent thought that it wore "an unconstitutional aspect". However, these obstacles were overcome, and the foundation stone of the United Services Club was laid in March, 1817.[1]

The employment of the army in connection with the suppression of riots did not add to its popularity in the country, but in the absence of any regular police force to cope with the disturbances, there was no alternative to calling out the troops, unless arson, pillage and the destruction of property were to be permitted to continue unchecked. The nation was passing through a difficult phase in its political and economic history, and it was useless to expect political leaders of the Tory party, like Lord Liverpool and Lord Sidmouth, to see that some changes must be made in the old order of things, even if they could not go far in the direction of meeting the wishes of Orator Hunt, and the theories expounded in Cobbett's *Political Register*.

On the death of the Duke of York in 1827, George IV wished to become Commander-in-Chief himself, but

[1] Delavoye, *Life of the Lord Lynedoch*, pp. 746–66.

gave up the idea when faced with the opposition of Lord Liverpool, who called it a "preposterous" suggestion.[1] He eventually agreed to the appointment of the Duke of Wellington, who was then Master-General of the Ordnance and, in that capacity, a member of the Cabinet. The Duke objected to the heavy reductions which were being made in the strength of the army. He considered that it was insufficient in strength to carry out the work it was called upon to perform, but, although he became Prime Minister in 1828, the establishment fell to 81,000 at home when he went out of office two years later, and rose again to 88,000 in 1831 in consequence of events in Belgium.[2] In 1827 Canning's government discussed a proposal to abolish the office of Commander-in-Chief and to appoint a Minister for War, with a Military Secretary, whose position would be equal to that of Commander-in-Chief in all but name. The plan was dropped after Canning's death in the August of that year.[3]

What has been described as "the greatest and most far-reaching military reform since Oliver Cromwell died, and his local constabulary perished with him", was brought about by the establishment of the Metropolitan Police in 1829.[4] It was held by some to be equivalent to the setting-up of another military force, which could interfere with the liberty of the subject, and was described,

[1] Croker, *Correspondence and Diaries*, I, p. 360.
[2] Fortescue, XI, p. 433. It may be noted that at the time of the crisis connected with the Reform Bill in 1832 it was doubtful if there were sufficient troops to hold London and other cities if the population had resorted to civil resistance.
[3] Moore Smith, *Life of Lord Colborne*, pp. 251-2: and Sir W. Napier, *Life*, I, p. 370.
[4] Fortescue, XI, p. 105.

as the army had been in years gone by, as "arbitrary, unconstitutional and extortionate".[1] Seven years later, Hume moved in Parliament for a reduction of the army establishment because, he argued, the police force made it unnecessary to retain the army on its previous scale. The institution of the County and Borough Police in 1856 and of the Irish Constabulary in 1836, in addition to those in London, relieved the army of many duties in connection with the maintenance of internal order which it had hitherto performed in the absence of any properly organised police service. There was much to be said in favour of the argument that these bodies of constabulary were akin to the army because they were armed to some extent, and disciplined in much the same way as the regular soldiers were. The adoption of a Free Trade policy in 1846 by Sir Robert Peel put an end to the army's employment on preventive duty.

In the foregoing pages, we have traced the steps by which the army was placed upon a constitutional basis after the Revolution of 1688, and the general attitude of Parliament to it during the eighteenth and beginning of nineteenth centuries. While the settlement of 1689 made it impossible for a standing army to exist again in this country without the annual approval of Parliament, and thus ameliorated the internal political situation, it had its repercussions on the conduct of foreign policy. In peace, as has been seen, the army was greatly diminished. In war it had to be hastily enlarged. Such a state of affairs was dangerous to the country. It was amply proved, for

---

The Times of October 2nd, 1830, in regard to a meeting of parishioners of St George the Martyr, Southwark. William Cobbett called the force the "half-military police", q.v. Political Register, June 22nd, 1833.

instance, by the events which followed the Treaty of Ryswick when Spain fell under the power and influence of France. The outbreak of war against the North American colonies, and the commencement of the long conflict in Europe in 1793, found the country embarking on international struggles with land forces that were both inadequate and unready. The same difficulty had to be faced in 1854, at the commencement of the Crimean War, and might have arisen again in 1870, had not both the French and German governments then agreed to respect Belgian neutrality in accordance with the Treaty of 1839. If war had broken out between France and Germany in 1887, this country would have had great difficulty in fulfilling her obligations under that Treaty owing to her military situation.

So far as the army itself was concerned, the system inaugurated as a consequence of the Revolution had a baneful effect. It meant that the uncertainty as to its future, which arose from the fact that Parliament's sanction for its existence had to be obtained annually, provided an excuse for paying little or no attention to the provision of comforts for the soldiers, and for failing to create any proper administrative system. The country at large took but little interest in the efficiency of the army, being content to see that the cost of its upkeep was kept as low as possible. Blackstone expressed the opinion that there should be "no separate camp, no barracks, no inland fortresses"[1], while Sir James Mackintosh rejoiced in the fact that "the Revolution bent the neck of military power under the yoke of Law, and rendered armies the creatures of Parliament, made and destroyed by its breath". An

[1] *Commentaries*, ed. 1766, I, p. 413.

unfortunate result was that the opening of every campaign found the country unprepared for war. The forces in being were ill-trained and ill-equipped, while the auxiliary services did not exist. The consequent expenditure of blood and money was unnecessarily high, but many years were to pass before it was accepted as the simple truth that the army must be ready to take the field, prepared in every respect, at the opening stage of a war. This axiom which seems so elementary to-day was not recognised in the eighteenth century. The army could perish in peace, and yet be trusted to extricate the country from military difficulties arising out of wars into which it had not led the nation.

CHAPTER III

THROUGHOUT the seventeenth and eighteenth centuries, the army suffered from the lack of any proper system of administration. Nor, indeed, was this serious defect remedied in an adequate manner until the latter half of last century. The system, if indeed it can be called a system at all, which had developed by the time of the French wars of 1793–1815, was the result of years of haphazard growth and was practically unworkable. If an officer were appointed to the command-in-chief, he was the nominee of the King, who in theory administered the army. Orders and regulations were issued by the Secretary-at-War. The Master-General of the Ordnance issued *matériel* and supervised the personnel of the artillery and engineers. The War Department was charged with the care of the cavalry and infantry. The Home Office was responsible for the militia and the volunteer corps of horse and foot. Boards of general officers were appointed to consider and advise on matters of importance to the army. The Treasury managed the transport and supply services. The office of Paymaster-General was much desired as a lucrative post, giving ample opportunity for self-enrichment to the holder. There were separate establishments for England and Scotland prior to 1707, and for Ireland until the Act of Union was passed by Pitt in 1800. These arrangements did not redound to the credit of the country, and complicated the difficulties of administering the army, both in peace and war. To understand subsequent developments of Parliament's efforts to obtain unfettered control of the army, it is necessary to consider the origin and growth of some of these offices. Like many other institutions in this country, the office of Secretary-at-War developed from small beginnings, gathering attributes to itself as time went on. Apparently the appointment came into being about the time of the Restoration, when the holder of the office became the Secretary of the Commander-in-Chief, and was subordinate to him. The Secretary's commission bound him to obey the orders of the Sovereign and of the Commander-in-Chief, and not those of Parliament. He was a civilian, but accompanied the Commander-in-Chief to the seat of war in the event of hostilities taking place. He conducted the Commander-in-Chief's correspondence. In 1670 the duty of attending the Commander-in-Chief in the field came to an end, but the Secretary-at-War's powers increased as no successor to Monk, who died in that year, was appointed. The business of the army had to be carried on, and the Secretary-at-War became responsible for movements, quarterings and reliefs. In William III's time he countersigned parliamentary estimates and issued orders for the Commander-in-Chief, all commissions and pay warrants passing through his hands. His duties were extended still further in Queen Anne's reign, when he took charge of military questions in the House of Commons, thus becoming a political officer without being a member of the ministry. The ultimate responsibility for the army still rested on the shoulders of the Secretary of State charged with the administration of domestic affairs, because the Secretary-at-War had no constitutional authority. From being the clerk to the Commander-in-Chief, he thus gradually became the recognised but not authorised representative of the army in Parliament, and the channel of communication between the King and the land forces. The position was most unsatisfactory. In 1779 Jenkinson declined to answer a question put to him by Fox in the House of Commons on the ground that he was not a minister and could not be expected "to have a competent knowledge of the destination of the army, and how the war was to be carried on". If important matters could be treated in this manner in the House of Commons by the Secretary-at-War, an effort had to be made to define his position and his responsibilities. Accordingly, under a measure, known as Burke's Act for Economical Reform,[1] which finally passed through Parliament in 1782, the government took over financial questions, which had been managed hitherto by the regimental commanders. The Secretary-at-War became definitely responsible for the financial and civil business of the army, and for the preparation of the estimates to be laid before Parliament. When supplies had been voted, he transmitted them to the Paymaster-General, who was responsible for their disbursement. The Secretary-at-War settled all accounts relating to expenditure within a definite period. He remained subordinate to the Cabinet, but although he was not a Cabinet minister,[2]

---

[1] 23 George III, c. 50.

[2] William Windham became a Cabinet minister in 1794 as Secretary-at-War.

he could no longer deny responsibility to Parliament. In fact, he became the responsible military minister. He was the link between the Sovereign and the army. He had nothing to do with the artillery and the engineers, nor with the supply of *matériel*, all of which remained under the supervision of the Master-General of the Ordnance, who also provided munitions for the navy. The Master-General was usually a soldier of distinction and a member of the Cabinet, but without responsibility for the military policy of the government, of which he was a member. His opinion, when asked, was given as his own personal opinion.[1]

The number of Secretaries of State has varied from time to time. There were two prior to 1708, when a third was added to manage the affairs of Scotland after the passing of the Act of Union. In 1746 the number dropped to two again. Twenty-one years later there was a Secretary for the Northern Department, and a Secretary for the Southern Department. The former was charged with this country's relations with the Northern powers, while the latter handled questions concerning the Southern powers, and, as a rule, Irish, Colonial and domestic affairs, including matters affecting the army. In 1768 Colonial problems, including the American War, were put in the charge of a third Secretary, but a reduction to two was made again in 1782. It was then decided to have a Foreign Secretary and a Home Secretary, Domestic, Irish and Colonial administration falling to the latter.

In 1794 a further change was made on account of circumstances arising out of the war with France. Pitt, faced with difficulties both abroad and at home, desired to

[1] The Master-General ceased to be a member of the Cabinet after 1828.

strengthen the political foundation upon which his government rested. With this object in view, the Duke of Portland and some of his Whig supporters joined a reconstituted ministry in that year. In this government, the office of Secretary of State for War appeared for the first time, an important step because it placed the army in the hands of a person holding office of the highest ministerial rank, and charged with definite responsibilities to Parliament. Nevertheless, no definite allotment of duties was made, and no clear line of demarcation was drawn showing, for instance, where the duties of the Secretary of State for Home Affairs, and of the Secretary of State for War, began and ended. The militia was still controlled by the former department. The Secretary of State for War was charged with questions affecting the military policy of the country; the amount of force to be maintained, subject to the approval of the Cabinet; the granting of commissions; the gazetting of promotions; the allotment and movement of troops on colonial and foreign service; and the general conduct of warlike operations.[1] Amidst all the vagueness of his position, there is no lack of proof that the planning and control of operations overseas formed part of his duties.[2] The Commander-in-Chief and the Secretary-at-War were expected to provide the means for carrying out these operations. Yet another change was made in 1801, when the business of the Colonies was transferred from the Home Department to that of the Secretary of State for War, who thus became the Secretary of State for War and the Colonies. This important alteration was made because

[1] Anson, *Law and Custom of the Constitution*, II, Pt I, pp. 166, 194.
[2] Furber, *Henry Dundas, 1st Viscount Melville*, pp. 95–125.

the army was engaged to a great extent in active operations in the West Indies. This distribution of duties remained in force till 1854.[1] The changes made in that year will be described in due course.

It is now necessary to consider briefly the office of principal command of the army before passing on to notice its relationship to that of the Secretary-at-War. The office has been known under a variety of titles such as Captain-General, Field-Marshal on the Staff, General Commanding-in-Chief, and Commander-in-Chief. After the Restoration, the King was in supreme control of the army, which was paid out of his Privy Purse, a system which continued until approval was given by Parliament for the maintenance of a standing army. Under Charles II, General Monk, who became Duke of Albemarle, was appointed Commander-in-Chief with very extensive powers in regard to such matters as the strength of the army, the granting of commissions, and the drawing up of articles of war. He was practically supreme in all military matters subject to the Sovereign's orders.[2] After his death, no Commander-in-Chief was appointed except when the country was engaged in military operations, the King retaining control in his own hands. During Queen Anne's reign, the Duke of Marlborough requested her to appoint him Captain-General of the Forces for life, but she refused to do so. It is probable that suspicions of his motives were aroused in political circles but, in any case, it was unusual to appoint a Commander-in-Chief when

[1] After 1815 the Secretary of State devoted more and more time to the Colonies until 1854 when a fourth Secretary of State was appointed with exclusive charge of the war.
[2] Fortescue, I, p. 309.

the country was not at war. Parliament decided in 1789 that the appointment of a Commander-in-Chief was unnecessary in peace, and the Secretary-at-War, who was responsible to Parliament, continued to issue orders and regulations to the army, subject to the controlling authority of a Secretary of State, who was the Home Secretary up to 1794 when a Secretary of State for War was appointed. These arrangements were not conducive to the good discipline of the army, as the Secretary-at-War was a politician, and subject to great political pressure on any question in which patronage played a part. Officers found that they could bring influence to bear on the Secretary-at-War by making use of their friends in Parliament, and regulations were set at nought with impunity by those who chose to neglect their duties. On the outbreak of the war with France in 1793, Lord Amherst was appointed Commander-in-Chief and charged with the supervision of matters of purely military administration. The Adjutant-General and Quartermaster-General's departments were both transferred to his office from that of the Secretary-at-War. In 1799 it was decided that all questions of discipline and regulations should pass through the Adjutant-General's office, while moves and quarters were handled by the Quartermaster-General. A War Office clerk was selected to act as the Commander-in-Chief's military secretary.

With the appointment of the Duke of York as Field-Marshal Commanding-in-Chief in 1795, a new era in the history of the British army was inaugurated. He created a headquarters staff. He secured control of almost the whole of the military forces, but not of those outside the United Kingdom as officers in command abroad reported to the Secretary of State. All promotions except to the highest posts, which were supervised by the Cabinet, passed into his hands. The discipline of the army was improved. A small addition to the pay of the privates in the line regiments was granted in 1797, the year of the mutinies in the fleet at Spithead and the Nore. Two years later, a school for officers was opened at High Wycombe, a plan which was denounced as "a step towards withdrawing the officer from civil society and making him a creature of the Crown", a phrase smacking of the political clap-trap of the time of William III. The Duke of York appointed a military officer in place of the civilian clerk to act as his military secretary, and gave his office an establishment which remained almost unchanged until the appointment of Commander-in-Chief was abolished in 1904. In 1805 all questions connected with the discipline of the army were placed under the Commander-in-Chief. Thus, it became unnecessary for the Secretary-at-War to have any connection with officers, a step in organisation which helped to end the evils arising from back-door political intrigues in favour of, or against, this or that officer. No officer was allowed to enter into direct correspondence with the Commander-in-Chief, the channel of communication through commanding officers being rigidly enforced.

Unfortunately, no definition of the powers of the Commander-in-Chief was made at the time, and nothing was done to indicate his sphere of duty apart from that of the Secretary-at-War. This failure to regulate their respective positions was the cause of many difficulties, and was the origin of the dual control which continued until 1870. Nevertheless, the revival of the office of Commander-in-Chief, the appointment of a Secretary of State for War, and the abolition of a separate Irish establishment after the passing of the Act of Union, were three definite steps towards a better system of administration. In so far as they affected the army, the most important at the time was the appointment of a Commander-in-Chief. This appointment definitely revived the King's personal control of the army, and considerably diminished the power of the Secretary-at-War, who was the representative of Parliament. However, the failure of the government to allot their respective duties, together with those of the Secretary of State for War, left the way open to much misunderstanding and mismanagement between these three officers. There was nothing to prevent the Secretary of State from moving troops about as he liked, a fact of which full advantage was taken. There was no system under which proposals for military operations had to be referred to the Commander-in-Chief for his advice and opinion. Whether he and the Master-General of the Ordnance were consulted or not, depended entirely on the whims of the ministers, many of whom had their own special ideas as to how the war should be conducted regardless of difficulties and objections which competent soldiers might have pointed out.[1]

The mistakes made by ministers in regard to the actual conduct of the war, and their failure to seek and take advice as to the strategy of the various campaigns and expeditions in different quarters of the globe upon which they embarked, are matters for purely military histories

[1] *Cornwallis Correspondence*, II, p. 336. Cornwallis' letter dated March 31st, 1798. He was Master-General of the Ordnance and in the Cabinet at the time.

rather than for these pages. More pertinent is the study of the relations between the two offices of Commander-in-Chief and Secretary-at-War. They are illustrative of the confusion which arose from the uncertainty as to their duties. For instance, in 1799, the Duke of York as Commander-in-Chief considered that he should have complete control of all the branches of the military service, including that of finance. William Windham, who was then Secretary-at-War, refused to agree to this proposal. A compromise was reached to the effect that all financial questions were to be left with the Secretary-at-War. The Commander-in-Chief was to control all questions of military discipline, regulations, movements and quarterings. This agreement was a temporary solution, but effected no definite settlement as the question was re-opened about ten years later after the resignation of the Duke of York in consequence of the scandals connecting his name with that of Mrs Mary Ann Clark. He was succeeded by General Sir David Dundas, "the precise and buckram Dundas" as Lord Cornwallis once called him.[1] Dundas' view was that the Secretary-at-War was in the same position to the Commander-in-Chief as he was to the King when the latter commanded the army in person. The Commander-in-Chief represented the King and, accordingly, the Secretary-at-War was subordinate to the Commander-in-Chief. He argued that the Secretary-at-War was only empowered to see that the accounts of the army were properly balanced, and that the law between civilians and soldiers was observed. Lord Palmerston, who was Secretary-at-War, replied in a lengthy memorandum upon "the office of Secretary-at-War

[1] *Cornwallis Correspondence*, I, p. 202.

with reference to the General Commanding-in-Chief"
in which he explained the relative positions of the two
officers.[1]

"Power", he wrote, "cannot be vested where there is no
responsibility, or responsibility imposed where authority does
not exist. The Legislature has imposed a responsibility upon
the Secretary-at-War from which he cannot discharge himself, and it would be placing him in a position perfectly
anomalous, and unknown to any office in the constitution, to
deprive him of that independence by which alone he can
secure to himself the power of faithfully performing his duty.
The office of Secretary-at-War has existed in point of fact,
and has been considered in point of law, as a sort of barrier
between the military authority of the officer in command of
the army and the civil rights of the people, and as a civil and
constitutional check on the expenditure of the money granted
by Parliament for the maintenance of the army."

He considered that the Secretary-at-War as the controller of finance was entitled to issue orders to the army.
The Commander-in-Chief would not tolerate this view.
The position thus reached was that the Commander-in-
Chief considered that the War Office should be subordinate to the Horse Guards, while the Secretary-at-War was
of the opinion that the Horse Guards should be subordinate to the War Office. This issue was to be raised from time
to time during the course of the next seventy or eighty
years, but, for the moment, it was settled by a Minute of
the Prince Regent in Council in May, 1812. The views of
the Secretary-at-War were generally upheld, but he was
instructed to show all orders to the Commander-in-Chief
prior to publication. If there was a matter in dispute upon
which no agreement could be reached, it was to be re-

[1] Clode, II, pp. 698–714.

ferred for decision to the First Lord of the Treasury, the Chancellor of the Exchequer and the Secretary of State for War and the Colonies.[1] These complications can be traced to the same foundation. It was the failure to allocate the duties and responsibilities of the various offices at the time of the reshuffling of portfolios in 1794, when an opportunity occurred to lay down some logical plan for the distribution of duties between the Secretary of State for War, the Secretary-at-War and the Commander-in-Chief. The office of Commander-in-Chief had only been revived the year before. The Secretary-at-War had his charter in precedent and Burke's Act of 1783. The Secretary of State for War was a new creation. However, nothing was done. Perhaps, nothing could be done, but it is noteworthy that the sixth report of the Commissioners of Military Enquiry had drawn attention to the lack of instructions for the guidance of the Secretary-at-War in the execution of his duties. The Commissioners state that they gathered that

at the periods when there was no Commander-in-Chief, the Secretary at War exercised a greater control in the discipline of the army, and a greater degree of patronage than he has done since.

They considered that his duty was finance as opposed to discipline, which was a matter for the Commander-in-Chief, but that matters such as the apprehension and escort of deserters, for instance, were the business of the War Office.[2]

This definition of the duties of these two high officers of State was in agreement with the generally accepted

---

[1] Clode, II, pp. 714–23.
[2] Printed by Order of Parliament June 25th, 1808.

view, difficult though it may have been for Commanders-in-Chief to acquiesce in the situation. It was in keeping with the trend of political thought as it had developed since the settlement of 1689. The position of the Secretary-at-War had been consolidated by Burke's Act, which cast upon him the responsibility of preparing and presenting estimates to Parliament, and of being responsible to Parliament for the financial business of the army. Pitt had made his Secretary-at-War a Cabinet minister just as he had the new Secretary of State for War. The Commander-in-Chief was not in the Cabinet and had no share in the responsibilities of the ministers. He was not answerable for any item of expenditure, provided he had obtained the concurrence of the Secretary-at-War. At the same time, the department of the Commander-in-Chief was not under the Secretary-at-War, who was only competent to observe on charges in the Commander-in-Chief's accounts or on proposals made by his office which seemed likely to result in possibly unnecessary expenditure. In any difference of opinion, the Secretary-at-War could always refer to the Board of Treasury or to the Cabinet.

Such a chaotic state of affairs at the apex of the administrative organisation was bound to have a deleterious effect on the army as a whole, and its deplorable condition after Waterloo is well known to students of English history. The main responsibility for the parlous state into which the army had been allowed to fall rested on Parliament, because an alteration of these conditions involved the expenditure of money which it was averse to asking the country to provide. Apart from the actual condition of the troops, the organisation at army headquarters in London remained unchanged. No steps were taken, after the end of the war in 1815, to improve and simplify the complicated organisation by which the army was administered. There were some thirteen different offices in which its business was conducted. Each was independent of the other. Each addressed letters to the other. There was no fountain-head to express the collective wisdom of the army upon any military problem. The Commander-in-Chief still had to communicate with the Master-General of the Ordnance on questions affecting the artillery or the engineers. If it was a question concerning the militia or the volunteers, or the employment of regular troops in aid of the civil power, he had to refer to the Home Office. The Treasury remained responsible for supply and transport. The Judge-Advocate-General advised on courts-martial and questions of discipline. The Secretary of State for War and the Colonies had to be consulted about the colonial garrisons. The Secretary-at-War represented the Commander-in-Chief in Parliament. In addition to these departments, there were the Controllers of Military Accounts, the Board of General Officers, the Army Medical Board, the Commissaries of Barracks, the Commissary-General of Musters, two Paymasters-General, and the Commissioners of Chelsea Hospital. It was not astonishing that such an array of unco-ordinated departments led to confusion, and to the production of an administrative system which was antiquated and inefficient.

A brief comparison with the navy is not without interest. The Admiralty, in which the whole business of the navy is now centred, at first was only concerned with larger questions of military control. It represented the ancient office of the Lord High Admiral, who was the

King's lieutenant for sea affairs. During the Commonwealth and Protectorate, a commission was appointed to
discharge the duties of the Lord High Admiral's office.
After the Restoration the Duke of York became Lord
High Admiral, but the office was put into commission
again after the Revolution of 1688. The civil business of
the navy was conducted by the Navy Board, which was
originally established by Henry VIII in 1546. With minor
modifications, these arrangements remained in force until
1832, when the consolidation of all naval business under
the Board of Admiralty was carried out by Sir James
Graham. At one period, prior to 1832, there were no less
than fifteen departments responsible for various branches
of naval business, and as in the case of the army offices,
they were housed under separate roofs with the conse-
quential loss of efficiency in administration. In the
eighteenth century, "gentlemen of parliamentary influence" were members of the Board of Admiralty and
frequently ignored the advice of experienced seamen,
when called upon to settle technical naval questions.
Secretaries of State issued orders to Admirals without
consulting the Board. In fact, therefore, for many years,
the navy laboured under difficulties which were not dis-
similar to those which confronted the sister service. In
some respects, however, the navy was clearly more
fortunate than the army. It was not so unpopular with
the politicians and, as a consequence, it had not to be re-
constructed from its foundations at the commencement
of every war. A definite nucleus always remained upon
which to develop.[1] For instance, in 1698, when the army

[1] Hannay, *Short History of the Royal Navy*; Richmond, *National Policy
and Naval Strength*.

was cut down to a strength of seven thousand men, the fleet was maintained at fifteen thousand.

The state of affairs in the army eventually led to the appointment of a Commission under the Duke of Richmond in 1833, to enquire into the practicability and expediency of consolidating the different departments connected with the civil administration of the army. As a result of its deliberations, the Committee proposed to amalgamate the offices of the Secretary-at-War, the Paymaster-General, the Commissariat, and certain minor departments, in one branch under a civilian, who was to be a member of the Cabinet, and to place the Master-General of the Ordnance under the Commander-in-Chief. These proposals were re-examined and adopted by a second Commission in 1837. No fewer than five Cabinet ministers were members under the chairmanship of Lord Howick, afterwards third Earl Grey, and a unanimous report was submitted. It advocated the centralisation of the civil administration of the army, and to ensure full and complete parliamentary control, it recommended that one estimate for all military expenditure should be prepared annually for submission to the House of Commons. Attention was directed to the fact that, with so many different departments, "the whole charge of the army is nowhere shown in one comprehensive review". Each department prepared its own estimates and submitted them independently, a method which was not in harmony with the soundest principles of finance. The report pointed out that the existing system caused the separation of the different branches of a common service, which were only connected by their subordination to the supreme authority of the government. The position of the Secretary-at-War was reviewed. His duties as explained in the report may be summarised as follows: the preparation of estimates and the general financial business of the army; the channel for publishing commissions in the *Gazette*, and the recording of promotions; parliamentary and legal proceedings in relation to the army; the superintendence of all matters relating to the apprehension and escort of deserters; the authority for all movements of troops; the channel of communication with the civil community; the protection of the civil subject from all improper military interference; the explanation and discussion of army business in the House of Commons.[1] He was not consulted as regards the "amount of force upon which the amount of expense mainly depends". The extent of the establishment was a matter for the government to determine. It was submitted direct to the King by the Commander-in-Chief, and subsequently communicated to the Secretary-at-War. He could suggest amendments to the establishment, but the government's decisions were naturally final. Even if the Secretary-at-War was a Cabinet minister, which was by no means the rule, he had no authority in this question, nor had he any responsibility for the efficiency of the army. The Commission of 1837 said that the difficulties between the Secretary-at-War and the Commander-in-Chief, to which attention had been drawn in 1812, still existed, and recommended that the former should be a Cabinet minister with immediate responsibility to Parliament. He should be the channel of communication from the Cabinet to the King on all questions

[1] Summarised from para. 2662, Minutes of Evidence Select Committee on Army and Navy Appointments (1833).

affecting the military establishments, and should correspond with the Commander-in-Chief on behalf of the
government. The Commission's recommendations on
this important aspect of their enquiry ran as follows:

If the military defence of the Empire is to be conducted
upon a footing of economy as well as of efficiency, it is
necessary that it should be managed upon a general and comprehensive system, having reference to the exigencies of the
Service both at home and abroad....It appears obviously
expedient that there should be some one member of the
Government particularly charged with the duty of exercising
a general superintendence, and control in all these matters,
and to whom it should more immediately belong to take the
pleasure of the Crown upon the annual establishment, and to
be responsible to Parliament for the advice so given by him.
The Secretary of State, to whom the civil administration of
our numerous colonies, with all their complicated interests,
is entrusted, cannot possibly give the attention to this subject
which it requires, and as it has been the practice to exclude
the Commander-in-Chief from the Cabinet, and, in a great
measure, to disconnect him from the Administration of the
day, the Secretary at War...seems to us to be the person
to whom the important duty of watching over the whole
military administration of the country should properly be
committed.[1]

Sir Henry Hardinge, who was then Commander-in-
Chief, gave evidence before the Commission. He was
opposed to any diminution of the power of the Commander-in-Chief in regard to approaching the King
direct, which he considered would be an encroachment
on the Royal Prerogative. He agreed with the Duke of
Wellington, who also appeared before the Commission,
in considering that the Secretary-at-War was paramount

[1] *Report*, p. 10.

in all questions of finance. The exclusive control over public money voted for military purposes rested with the Secretary-at-War.

"The Commander-in-Chief", said the Duke of Wellington in his evidence, "cannot, at this moment, move a corporal's guard from hence to Windsor without going to the civil department for authority. He must get a route.... The Secretary-at-War has a clear duty to perform. He has to take care that the votes of Parliament are not exceeded and that no expense is incurred by the Commander-in-Chief which is not necessary; in short, that no expense can be incurred without his consent."

Sir Henry Hardinge also made a statement in which he gave further views on the position of the Secretary-at-War whom he regarded as responsible for seeing that justice was done in any conflict between civilians and military. He considered that the separation of finance and discipline was as it ought to be. Finance was a matter for the House of Commons, while discipline and management were for the King as represented by the Commander-in-Chief. He held that the latter was an executive, and not a ministerial officer, whom it was important to keep clear of politics, by making him independent of whatever government was in office. The proceedings of this Commission have been reviewed at some length, because of the importance of the subject which was to be debated from this time onwards whenever the question of the reorganisation of the army was discussed. The intricate question of the relationship between the civil authority, as represented by a ministerial officer, and the military authority, as represented by the Commander-in-Chief, was not to be finally settled for more than half-a-century. Their respective responsibilities and duties formed the salient point in all discussions on the administration of the army.

On reviewing the Commission's report Lord Melbourne, the Prime Minister, consulted the Duke of Wellington, who expressed his hostility to the suggested establishment of a consolidated War Office. He held that the Sovereign was the head of the army, commanding it through the Commander-in-Chief, who had no power to move a man, nor to spend a penny without the approbation of the Secretary-at-War who, he wrote, would be a "new leviathan" if the suggested consolidation were carried out. Patronage and discipline were in the hands of the Commander-in-Chief, an arrangement which afforded some measure of protection against political influence. He considered that the Commissariat should remain under the Treasury, but the Master-General of the Ordnance occupied a different position. He had to work with both the navy and the army and was burdened with considerable financial responsibilities. He was generally a member of the Cabinet and a military adviser to the government. The Duke thought that the proposal of the Commission would make the Secretary-at-War absolute, as everything would pass under his control, and no Commander-in-Chief would be able to retain his position when confronted by a Secretary-at-War, who was a member of the Cabinet, with the House of Commons behind him. In short, the Duke of Wellington feared that the effective command of the army would be transferred from the Sovereign to the House of Commons, and that the work done by the Duke of York in rescuing the army from the evils of political interference would be destroyed. He wanted to protect the army, which he thought would be seriously injured if the House of Commons ever resumed any connection with its discipline.[1] The views of the army were in agreement with these opinions.

Parliamentary opinion was in favour of a measure making for some concentration of power. The multiplicity of offices, and the lack of any one authority to guide and control the all-too-numerous counsellors who each had a voice in the management of the army, were obvious sources of weakness in a vital part of the country's defences. It was felt that somebody ought to be responsible for plans and organisation, just as the Secretary-at-War was responsible for army finance. It was thought that the best solution would be to carry out the recommendations of the Commission by making one War Minister, who would ask Parliament for money and, at the same time, be charged with the whole management of army business. Lord Melbourne was prepared to recommend Queen Victoria to make some alteration in the direction proposed by the Commission. He informed her that he would submit a copy of the proposed Order in Council to her, so that she would know exactly "what the powers and duties are, which it is intended to transfer from the Secretary of State to the Secretary-at-War".[2] This proposed transfer of duties was probably due to the fact that the military side of the Secretary of State's office had been practically in abeyance since the end of the war in 1815. As has been pointed out already, the attention of that Secretary of State was almost solely devoted to the con-

[1] Clode, II, pp. 759–63.
[2] *Queen Victoria's Letters*, 1837–61, I, pp. 129–30.

sideration of problems connected with colonial administration. In the end, nothing was done, although five
Cabinet ministers had pledged themselves to the proposed
alteration by signing the report. No doubt the Duke of
Wellington's views contributed very largely to this result, because he occupied a unique position in the country,
where his opinion on military matters naturally carried
immense weight. The outbreak of the Crimean War in
1854, seventeen years afterwards, found the army with
the same departmental organisation that it had had at the
time of the battle of Waterloo, thirty-nine years earlier.

Before passing on to relate the radical changes in army
organisation, which were introduced in consequence of
the startling failures of the administrative machinery
which came to light in 1854, it will be convenient to refer
briefly to certain events which took place between the
accession of Queen Victoria to the throne in 1837 and the
commencement of the war against Russia in 1854. It has
been shown that recommendations to place the army
administrative system on a different footing were dis-
regarded but, as time went on, there was a slight re-
crudescence of interest in military affairs. The advent of
a young Sovereign to the throne was, perhaps, a reason
why changes in the army were difficult to make, and Lord
Melbourne as Prime Minister moved with the utmost
caution. In 1841, for instance, in writing to the Queen
about the case of Lord Cardigan, he warned her that if an
address for his removal from his regiment were moved in
the House of Commons, it would be difficult to resist,
"and nothing is to be more apprehended and deprecated
than such an interference of the House of Commons
with the interior discipline and government of the

army".[1] He, like the Duke of Wellington, feared a revival of the old system under which the grievances of officers were a means of bringing political pressure to bear upon the Secretary-at-War. The marriage of the Queen to Prince Albert of Saxe-Coburg in 1840 probably had a livening effect on the interest taken in military matters at the Court. The Prince made a profound and meticulous study of public business, and devoted much attention to the army, in common with the numerous other subjects which came to his notice. By training and tradition, he was naturally imbued with German views on constitutional questions. Nevertheless, in many of his memoranda on military matters, he voiced suggestions, such as the creation of an army reserve, and the need for the collective training of forces of all arms, to which the ministers of the day would have been wiser had they paid more heed.[2]

The Duke of Wellington succeeded Lord Hill as Commander-in-Chief in 1842, and held that office for the remaining ten years of his life. Although he pressed Sir Robert Peel, the Prime Minister, to make improvements in the army, no efforts were made to take up the question as seriously as the position of affairs demanded. The Prime Minister's opinion was that

We should best consult the true interests of the country by husbanding our resources in time of peace and—instead of a lavish expenditure on all the means of defence—by placing some trust in the latent and dormant energies of the nation, and acting upon the confidence that a just cause would rally a great and glorious people round the national standard and enable us to defy the menaces of any foreign power.[3]

[1] *Queen Victoria's Letters*, 1837–61, I, pp. 330 *et seq.*
[2] Martin, *Life of Prince Consort*, II, p. 436; III, p. 188.
[3] *Hansard*, CIX, p. 765.

Parliament was too deeply engaged in the consideration of such matters as the repeal of the Corn Laws, the employment of women and children in coal mines, factory legislation, and the Chartist agitation. However, a measure known as the Army Service Act came into force in 1847, under which ten or twelve years' service was allowed with a right to re-engage for a similar period so as to qualify for pension. No effort was made to round off this reform by creating an Army Reserve to be called up in case of national emergency. The Army Service Act, and the re-raising of the militia in 1852, in circumstances which will be briefly described, were the most definite signs that public interest in military matters was awakening.

The Radical school of politicians still believed in the views held in the middle of the eighteenth century about a standing army and about the iniquities of barracks.[1] Parliament was apt to look at matters from a "cold and thrifty" point of view, and to think more of the importance of placating the taxpayers than of making adequate provision for the military services. The Duke of Wellington was despondent about the condition of the national defences, but failed to arouse the parliamentary leaders to a sense of the seriousness of the situation. He considered that the country was in a defenceless position, and that the means available for conducting operations in Canada in 1837, for example, were insufficient. What troops there were had too much work to do, and no adequate force existed in the event of the country being engaged in a European struggle. Prominent politicians were divided on the question. Lord Clarendon and Lord

[1] Morley, *Life of Cobden*, Popular ed., pp. 481, 507.

Palmerston agreed with the Duke. Lord Chancellor Cottenham was opposed to any steps being taken which would prove expensive. Lord John Russell adopted an attitude of neutrality. Lord Grey considered that the Duke of Wellington himself was the obstacle to any improvement in the situation.[1] In 1847 part of a confidential letter addressed by the Duke to Field-Marshal Sir John Burgoyne was published in the *Morning Chronicle*. In it, he said that he had made fruitless efforts to get governments to attend to the inadequacy of the country's defences, and that in his opinion, the whole of the south coast was open to invasion, and without means of opposing a hostile force.[2] This outspoken statement displeased the Radicals, and Cobden, for instance, seized the opportunity, given by a speech at Manchester, to pour ridicule on armaments, and to attack the Duke of Wellington in vulgar terms for calling attention to the parlous state of the country's defences. It was an unfortunate moment to choose in which to develop the fondly cherished but misleading argument that the peace, which had existed since Waterloo, would continue for ever, and that governments had no further need to maintain standing armies. Events on the continent of Europe were causing anxiety to this country. There were revolutionary movements in France, Austria, Spain, Hungary, Italy and Poland. The abdication of King Louis-Philippe, and the declaration of Prince Louis Napoleon as President-elect of the French Republic in 1848, alarmed public opinion in England where doubts arose as to the future political relations of the two countries. The situation did not improve at

[1] Greville, III, p. 76.
[2] Wrottesley, *Life of Sir J. Burgoyne*, I, p. 444.

first when the Prince-President became the Emperor Napoleon III in December, 1852.

In the preceding February, Lord John Russell's government brought in a bill to reorganise the militia, but was defeated on a motion by Lord Palmerston to omit the word "local" from the title of the bill, so as to make the force available as a reserve for the regular army. The government resigned. Lord Derby formed a new administration, and introduced fresh proposals making the militia liable for service in any part of the United Kingdom. It was to be recruited by voluntary enlistment, the ballot being retained for emergencies. On June 15th of that year, in his last speech in the House of Lords, the Duke of Wellington gave his approval to the measure. He said that the country had never had a proper peace establishment, and that it was now necessary to form such an establishment upon the militia. As to the regular army, there had not been for the last ten years "more men than enough to relieve the sentries on duty at your stations in different parts of the world".[1] The opponents of preparedness in national defence considered that the militia system was calculated to foster and strengthen an aristocratic system, and to degrade the mass of the people. They pinned their faith to the efficiency of the navy as an adequate defence for the country, without the assistance of land forces.[2]

The Duke of Wellington died at Walmer Castle on September 14th, 1852, and the important task of choosing his successor as Commander-in-Chief had to be faced. His view, which he had expressed in 1850, was that the Prince Consort should become Commander-in-Chief, so that

[1] *Speeches in Parl.* II, p. 734.   [2] Morley, *Life of Cobden*, pp. 583–4.

the attachment of the army to the Crown would be maintained and emphasised by the close bonds of union that would spring from such an appointment. The Prince Consort doubted whether he would be acting within the constitution if he accepted the command. The Duke's reply was to the effect that, as the power of the democracy grew stronger, the power of the executive grew weaker, and that it was of the utmost importance to the throne and constitution that the command of the army should remain in the hands of the Sovereign, and not fall into the hands of the House of Commons.[1] This suggestion was investigated after the Duke's death, but Prince Albert finally decided that it was better for him to decline the office of Commander-in-Chief, because of the difficulties which would arise in the event of his having to direct operations against subjects of the Crown. Moreover, he had no experience of military operations.[2] "Lord Derby", said the Prince, with whom the subject was discussed, "seemed relieved by my explanation." Lord Derby then suggested that the Duke of Cambridge should be appointed, but this proposal was rejected on the grounds of his youth and lack of seniority. It was felt that he would be ineffective in a position involving great responsibilities, at a time when the death of Wellington was likely to open the way for an attack on the whole question of army organisation. The choice eventually fell on Lord Hardinge, a soldier who combined distinction in the field with experience of administrative work in Parliament and at the Board of Ordnance.

---

[1] Maxwell, *Life of Wellington*, II, pp. 370–1.
[2] Martin, *Life of the Prince Consort*, II, pp. 252–62, 263; Parker, *Life of Sir James Graham*, II, p. 436.

The new Commander-in-Chief had to meet a position of peculiar difficulty. Some political leaders still believed that the long peace in Europe would remain unbroken. Others were fearful of the result of the new orientation given to affairs in France by the changes which followed the events of 1848–52. Lord Derby's Chancellor of the Exchequer, Mr Benjamin Disraeli, thought that Lord Hardinge was "very prone to expenditure".[1] The Chancellor's wish was to produce a successful and popular Budget, and he did not look forward with pleasure to any increase in the estimates for what he once called the "damned defences".[2] The correspondence of the Queen and the Prince Consort with both Lord Derby and his successor, Lord Aberdeen, prove with what anxiety the problem of defence was considered, and with what a true appreciation the enfeebled condition of the country's military resources was regarded, in the highest places. For instance, on October 23rd, 1852, the Queen wrote to Lord Derby, asking what was the position of the national defences, and suggesting that he should call for a report from the Commander-in-Chief, the Master-General of the Ordnance, and the First Lord of the Admiralty. "It will soon be necessary", she wrote, "to consider what will have to be done for the future to complete the various plans." A few days later, the Prince Consort wrote, saying that the Queen wanted to know the situation, and advocated a consultation between the Horse Guards and the Board of Ordnance. The following year, in writing to Lord Palmerston, who was then at the Home Office, the Queen commented on the want of arms for the militia

[1] *Disraeli's Life*, iii, p. 392.
[2] *Ibid.* iii, p. 439.

and complained that she was always told that they would be provided immediately. In 1854 she urged Lord Aberdeen, the Prime Minister, to proceed to the augmentation of the army.[1]

The evil results of a system which put economy before efficiency in a matter of vital national importance, were not to be swept away by the writing of memoranda and fugitive discussions in Parliament, where a policy of drift was pursued, in preference to taking steps to put the army on a satisfactory basis. It was fortunate that peace lasted long enough to enable Lord Hardinge, with the assistance of Sidney Herbert, the Secretary-at-War, to carry out a partial re-armament of the artillery with guns of a more recent design than those of the Waterloo pattern with which they were still equipped. At the same time, means were found to begin equipping the infantry with the Minié rifle in place of the old-fashioned musket, popularly known as "Brown Bess". Neither the public, nor the army as a whole, realised the importance of these changes in armament. Another innovation, in the shape of the establishment of a "camp of exercise" at Chobham Common in 1853, may be noted in passing.

The ability of Lord Hardinge and the activity of Herbert were unable to remedy the faults of the system they had inherited before the storm burst upon them. The Crimean War broke out in March, 1854, and the nation had to bear the shame, and the army the burden, of thirty-nine years of neglect and apathy. In addition to reductions in strength, efficiency had been allowed to suffer because Parliament took no profound interest in the army. Troops were scattered far and wide. Ten thousand pen-

[1] *Queen Victoria's Letters*, 1837–61, II, pp. 481–3, 536.

sioners represented the only tangible reserve.[1] Trained staff officers were wanting. Transport and medical arrangements did not exist. Despite past experiences, notably in the Peninsular War, the Commissariat had been practically swept away on the recommendation of a Parliamentary Committee of 1850, before which Lord Raglan, the Commander-in-Chief in the Crimea, had given evidence against the maintenance of a Commissariat Department in peace.[2] There was still the same interminable number of offices, each running its own branch without regard to what its next door neighbour was doing. The Commander-in-Chief related that he was never consulted by the Secretary of State on any subject connected with the war, and that he had never seen a single dispatch except those that had been published in the newspapers.[3] There was still the same circumlocution, the same masses of correspondence, the same lack of organisation, and the same absence of guidance and control. Lives were lost, and the country's substance wasted, while the nation was learning once again the lesson of unpreparedness for war. The old dispute about the position and powers of the Secretary-at-War was still unsettled. Lord Palmerston had suggested, at the time of the Duke of Wellington's death, that the appointment of Commander-in-Chief was vested in that Secretary. The Prince Consort did not agree, but said that doubts existed as to the person in whom the command of the army was vested in the case of a vacancy. The Secretary-at-War had authority in matters

[1] *Wolseley's Life*, p. 11.
[2] *Committee on Army and Ordnance Expenditure* (1850), H.C. 662, II, p. 240.
[3] Malmesbury, *Memoirs of an Ex-Minister*, p. 345.

of finance and nothing else, while the Commander-in-Chief had no authority to spend a penny without the concurrence of the Secretary-at-War.[1] The position remained obscure. The Secretary of State for War and the Colonies was still too pre-occupied with colonial affairs to represent army matters in the Cabinet, and his duties in this respect still awaited authoritative definition. The Secretary-at-War was not in the Cabinet, and the Queen was opposed to his admission to it. She told Lord Aberdeen, when he was forming his government towards the end of 1852, that "the Secretary-at-War ought properly to be left out of the Cabinet for the well working of the army", a view based, no doubt, on her fears, which developed as years went on, of the possible aggrandisement of civil as opposed to military authority in army matters.[2] The military member of the Cabinet was the Master-General of the Ordnance, but his position remained unaltered in that his opinions were personal, and he took no responsibility for the administration of the army. Such, in short, was the position when the war began. The failure of a long succession of Cabinets and Parliaments to reform the military machine, was to be brought home to the whole country with terrifying vividness in the course of the next few months. However, at the commencement of the campaign, a spirit of optimism prevailed, and the news from the seat of war lent some colour to the hope that the fall of Sebastopol would not be long delayed. In fact, people who ought to have known better, wrote letters expressing their satisfaction at the army being in so efficient a condition after the long

[1] *Queen Victoria's Letters*, 1836–61, II, p. 477.
[2] *Ibid.* II, p. 514.

years of peace, and commenting favourably upon the "celerity, energy and efficiency" displayed in the dispatch of the troops to the seat of war.[1] It was not long before the British public were profoundly shaken in the fatal complacency that had become a habit so far as military matters were concerned. Winter found the allied armies unprepared to face the rigours of the Crimean climate during the dark and stormy months, and the British troops had to endure almost incredible sufferings, which were denounced in no uncertain tones in the famous letters of Russell, *The Times'* correspondent with the army in the field. The archaic administrative machine, in which the right hand never knew what the left was doing, broke down at the moment when it ought to have been working at full speed, if it were to compete with the many urgent problems which a state of war was certain to create. Although steps had been taken to alleviate the situation at the seat of war in various directions, blame for the chaos which existed before Sebastopol and at home, had to be borne by the Headquarters Staff in the Crimea, and Lord Aberdeen's government in London. On the first night of the parliamentary session, which began in January, 1855, Roebuck gave notice of a motion for a committee, to enquire "into the condition of our army before Sebastopol, and into the conduct of those departments of the government, whose duty it has been to minister to the wants of that army". The motion was carried by a majority of 157 on the 30th of that month, and the government resigned. The Committee sat in

[1] Croker, *Correspondence and Diaries*, III, p. 326. Cf. Macaulay's letter on reading the *Inkerman Gazette*, in Trevelyan, *Life of Lord Macaulay*, ch. xiii.

almost continuous session from March to June. It is unnecessary to linger over its report, which blamed the late
government in a series of general statements. As a matter
of fact, Lord Aberdeen's administration was no more to
blame than any of its predecessors. As Mr Sidney Herbert
truly said, it was

> the fault of all Parties, all Administrations, every Parlia-
> ment.... At the commencement of the war we had to make
> means, and to create an Army and to use it at the same time.
> ...It is a difficulty which you have to encounter when you
> have to make an Army at the same time you are to use it.[1]

Meanwhile, Lord Palmerston had formed an administration in which Lord Panmure became Secretary of State
for War in succession to the Duke of Newcastle. In Lord
John Russell's government, as Fox Maule, he had been
Secretary-at-War from 1846 to 1852, being advanced to
Cabinet rank in 1849.[2] In 1852 he became President of
the Board of Control on Indian Affairs. After the change
of ministries in that year, he had remained out of office,
until Lord Palmerston called upon his services in February, 1855. He thus entered upon his new duties with considerable experience of public business, a matter of great
importance in view of the critical situation with which
the military departments were confronted. Partly as a
result of the unwieldy nature of its machinery, largely
because of the indifference with which all military questions had been treated since 1815, the old system of
administration had failed at a critical juncture. Something
had to be done, and done quickly, if the army in the field
was not to perish. It could not be left to save itself by its

---

[1] Stanmore, *Memoirs of Sidney Herbert*, I, pp. 239–40.
[2] *The Panmure Papers*, I, p. 28.

own exertions in a desolate land, where no material assistance could be obtained. To afford the help for which it had looked in vain during the first terrible winter, demanded the introduction of new men and new methods at home more than in the field, unless the country was prepared to countenance the sacrifice of the lives of its soldiers on the bare uplands of the Chersonese Peninsula.

The first step taken by the new government aimed at a consolidation of the offices concerned with military affairs. In the previous June, a step in this direction had been taken when the office of the Secretary of State for the Colonies was given a separate existence instead of remaining as a branch of the combined office of Secretary of State for War and the Colonies as it had been since the days of the Napoleonic wars. This rearrangement enabled the Secretary of State for War to devote his time and energy to the rapidly increasing business of the war. Under Lord Palmerston he was placed in authority over a number of the other departments, which had led a separate existence up to that time, while certain army business was transferred to his office from other departments of State. The Army Medical Board and the Board of General Officers passed under his control. The duty of providing clothing for the regiments was withdrawn from the colonels and undertaken by the government. The militia and yeomanry which had been transferred to the Secretary-at-War from the Home Office in 1852, were transferred in 1855 to the Secretary of State for War, a plan which was in full consonance with the wishes of the Queen. The Commissariat had been taken from the Treasury in the previous December. The Letters Patent of the Board of Ordnance, which dated back to the four-

teenth century, were revoked in May, 1855,[1] and its duties
were divided between the Commander-in-Chief and the
Secretary of State for War, greatly to the dislike of Lord
Raglan who had been Master-General since 1852. He
conscientiously believed that the change would not be
beneficial to the public.[2] The Commander-in-Chief became responsible for the administration of the Artillery
and the Engineers, while the Secretary of State undertook
the supervision of the civil side of the Board's activities.
Concurrently with his appointment as Secretary of State
for War, Panmure was appointed Secretary-at-War, and
was given a military officer junior to the Commander-in-
Chief to act as Secretary for Military Correspondence, a
post that developed in course of time into that of Permanent Under-Secretary of State for War. It may be
noted here that the historic office of Secretary-at-War
was abolished in 1863 when its duties and powers were
finally absorbed in that of the Secretary of State for War.[3]

The amalgamation of offices was thus carried out whilst
the country was engaged in a difficult campaign in a
distant land. The "old-fashioned departmentalism", to
quote a phrase of Lord Panmure, was swept away, and
replaced by a system which, it was hoped, would lead to
efficiency in the long run. There were difficulties and pre-
judices to overcome. The Queen had very decided views
on suggested changes in military matters, and impressed

[1] Cf. 18 and 19 Vic. c. 117. An Act for transferring to One of Her
Majesty's Principal Secretaries of State the Powers and Estates vested in
the principal Officers of the Ordnance. August 14th, 1855.

[2] *The Panmure Papers*, I, p. 203.

[3] 26 and 27 Vic. c. 12. Lord Panmure's speech on February 21st, 1856,
explaining the changes to the House of Lords is quoted in full in *The
Panmure Papers*, II, p. 117 n.

them on the Secretary of State. She was jealous of decisions which she thought in any way infringed her prerogatives. She disliked any interference in what she considered the special sphere of the Commander-in-Chief and did not fail to register her protest if she thought that her ministers neglected to supply her with full information on proposals in any way affecting the army. The appointment of an officer as Secretary for Military Correspondence introduced a military element in the Secretary of State's office, where civilians had always reigned supreme. The fact that this officer would probably handle correspondence emanating from the Commander-in-Chief, and quite conceivably communicate the Secretary of State's decisions, added to the jealousy already existing between the Horse Guards and Pall Mall.

It is in the actual terms of the patent appointing the Secretary of State for War that the source of much future trouble between the two offices can best be traced. The effect of the amalgamation of various departments was to concentrate the business of the army under two rival authorities. They were the Secretary of State, who thus became responsible for finance, clothing, and all the civil administration of the army, and the Commander-in-Chief, who exercised independent command of the army, handling such questions as discipline and promotion. Set out in these terms, the line of demarcation between their respective spheres of duty may seem clear. However, it must be remembered that considerable divergence of opinion existed as to where the line between the civil and the military authority was drawn. This point had been a matter of argument for many years. The truth is that their duties were never clearly defined. Although, no doubt, the concentration of offices marked a definite and necessary step towards an improved organisation in the future, the absorption of so much power by the Secretary of State tended to increase the difficulties. In theory, he was responsible for the manner in which the Commander-in-Chief fulfilled his duties, but it was no easy matter to lay down precise rules for the guidance of the Commander-in-Chief and the Secretary of State. Earlier in the year, before the fall of Lord Aberdeen's government, when a proposal to establish a board on the affairs of the army had been considered, the Queen had impressed on Lord Aberdeen how ambiguous and undefined the powers of the Commander-in-Chief were, and had asked that they should be clearly laid down.[1] Nothing was then done, on account of the change of government, but in 1855, a definite move was made by the Crown to re-assert its position in relation to the army. Prior to that date, the patent appointing the Secretary of State for War and the Colonies, was identical to those of the other Secretaries of State, whose duties were interchangeable, though for the sake of convenience, each Secretary had particular duties assigned to him. The patents were in general terms without limitations. The original patent for the Secretary of State for War contained no reservation, but, after the Board of Ordnance passed under his control in 1855, special reservations were added to it, a supplementary patent being issued in May of that year. This patent was revocable at the pleasure of the Crown, and while granting the Secretary of State the administration and government of the land forces, contained a reservation of all powers of command, discipline, appointments, and pro-

[1] *Queen Victoria's Letters*, 1837–61, III, pp. 89–90.

motions, which were vested in the hands of the Commander-in-Chief.[1] A patent drawn with these limitations on the powers of the Secretary of State was an
innovation, and did not help to clarify the situation. As
will be seen later on, considerable doubts existed as to the
exact bearing and results which were expected to follow
from its issue. It did nothing to improve the relationship
between the Horse Guards and the War Office. It is uncertain how far such a patent was required, as it did not
affect the Secretary of State's responsibility as the holder
of the seals which he received from the hands of the
Sovereign-in-Council. It was in no sense a final solution
of the problem, as the old objection to the Commander-
in-Chief being in any way departmentally subordinate
to the Secretary of State remained unsolved, while the
parliamentary view that all authority in army matters
must be exercised through a minister responsible to
Parliament, was upheld in many quarters. The general
feeling was that no member of Parliament should have
the patronage of the army in his hands, and that all
honours and rewards for military service should be in the
control of the Commander-in-Chief as the representative
of the Sovereign. In 1860, a Select Committee on Military Organisation, over which Sir James Graham presided, examined this question at considerable length. It
reported that previously no limitation had been placed
on the Secretary of State, and expressed the opinion that
no supplementary patent was required. The responsibility of the Secretary of State remained constitutionally
unchanged. It was pointed out that every public docu-

[1] See *Report of Select Committee on Military Organisation*, 1860: *Cardwell
at the War Office*, p. 235.

ment such, for instance, as an army commission signed by the Sovereign, has a Secretary of State's signature appended. Thus, while the Sovereign can do no wrong, the responsible adviser for every act is ascertained, and the minister must answer for what the Crown has done so long as he holds the seals of his office.

The Committee reviewed the relationship of the Commander-in-Chief and the Secretary of State. In his evidence, the Duke of Cambridge admitted, that in the case of a difference of opinion, a decision must rest with the Secretary of State

because the Secretary of State would, in the constitutional form, advise Her Majesty to take his opinion and not that of the Commander-in-Chief, so that it must naturally come to the decision of the Secretary of State.[1]

The Committee agreed with this statement, and considered that the reservation made in Lord Panmure's patent was inoperative. In fact, the Secretary of State was supreme in the control of the army. However, in a memorandum dated October 11th, 1861, drawn up by Sir George Cornewall Lewis, the then Secretary of State for War, and signed by the Queen, military command and discipline, appointments and promotions, were ordered to be vested in the Commander-in-Chief, subject to the general control of the Crown over the government of the army, and the responsibility of the Secretary of State for the exercise of the royal prerogative.[2] This document, which was never used, was lost for seven years, and both Commander-in-Chief and Secretary of State

---

[1] Minutes of Evidence 3889–3890, *Report of Committee of* 1860.
[2] Clode, II, 351. Verner, *Military Life of Duke of Cambridge*, I, pp. 112–13.

claimed to be supreme, an anomalous position which it was difficult to regulate.

If the relative positions of these two high officers of State, as they were in 1854 and 1868, are compared, it will be seen that in the interval the Commander-in-Chief had acquired the command of the army both at home and abroad, including the artillery and the engineers, and the control of all fortresses. At the same time, there had been a certain addition to the powers of the Secretary of State as a result of the concentration of the supply and finance departments. On the whole, the balance was in favour of the latter, upon whom the Commander-in-Chief was becoming gradually, and, perhaps, almost imperceptibly, more and more dependent, as the army could not exist without certain services which were entirely supervised by the parliamentary head of the War Office.[1]

[1] *Cardwell at the War Office*, pp. 14–15.

CHAPTER IV

The Duke of Cambridge as Commander-in-Chief; the Queen and the army; age of reform; rise of Prussia; Cardwell regime; Northbrook Committee; War Office and Horse Guards; reorganisation; opposition of the Commander-in-Chief; supremacy of the Secretary of State; Surveyor-General of Ordnance; office of Military Secretary; short service; abolition of purchase

LORD HARDINGE retired after the Peace of Paris, which brought the war to an end in 1856. His successor was George, Duke of Cambridge, the Queen's cousin. He was thirty-seven years of age, and had served in the recent campaign in Russia. Appointed as General Commanding-in-Chief, he was promoted Commander-in-Chief at the time of the Queen's Jubilee in 1887. Imbued with a strong sense of the desirability of upholding the royal prerogative, he had written a memorandum, during the previous year, supporting the point of view that finance and administration were the field of the Secretary of State, while discipline and command were matters for the Commander-in-Chief. He was tenacious of his opinions on such questions as length of service and promotion by seniority, and loved parades and set field days. He made submissions direct to the Queen, which ought to have passed through the hands of the ministers in the first place. The Queen considered his appointment as the only one it was possible to make, "though in some respects it may be a weakness for the Crown, it is a great strength for the army".[1] His conservatism in military matters, and his firm belief in the efficacy of his own ideas

[1] *Queen Victoria's Letters*, 1837–61, III, p. 254.

about the army, increased the difficulty of carrying out desirable and necessary reforms. In the course of his long tenure of office, he agreed to a great reorganisation of the army, to the abolition of purchase, and to certain other less sweeping changes, which followed as the logical development of Lord Cardwell's reforms. His personal views must have been strongly opposed to much in which he had to acquiesce, and probably nothing was more distasteful to him than the gradual but irresistible growth of the power of the Secretary of State, and, through him, of the supremacy of Parliament in military affairs. His loyalty to the traditional position of the Crown in regard to the army must have made him feel an absolute repugnance to the idea that the Commander-in-Chief, the representative of the Sovereign, was in any sense answerable for his acts to a political Secretary of State. His great desire was "to keep up that connecting link which binds the army to the Crown". He was so intensely conservative that he only agreed to alterations when he was convinced that they could be refused no longer.[1] He was out of harmony with the reformers, and detested what he called their "damned new-fangled methods".[2] He could never bring himself into real sympathy with the changes introduced from 1868 onwards. Nevertheless, once a decision in any matter was given against him, even if he doubted its wisdom, he did his best to carry out the alterations necessitated by the new order of things.

Lord Panmure's reforms had aggravated the long-standing quarrel between the War Office and the Horse Guards, and the advent of a Commander-in-Chief holding the views held by the Duke of Cambridge was un-

[1] *Wolseley's Life*, p. 234.   [2] *Ibid.* p. 114.

likely to diminish the friction already existing between the two offices. In June, 1858, the Commons resolved that the whole administration of the army should be placed under the sole authority of a single minister. The Queen and the Duke were opposed to any ideas involving the final subordination of the Commander-in-Chief to the Secretary of State, and she wrote to the Prime Minister, Lord Derby, explaining their uneasiness, though she did not contemplate

the possibility of any *real* attempt to divest the Crown of its prerogative in this instance. The army will not, she feels sure, stand it for a moment...if properly defined and explained, the House of Commons will not acquiesce in any such disloyal proceeding.[1]

Though the government of that day did not make any move in the matter, the time was fast approaching when this question was to be solved, and the House of Commons was to assert its determination to place its representative, the Secretary of State, in a position of absolute authority in regard to administration, though it was wisely content to leave questions of command in the independent and unbiased keeping of the Crown.

The pages of the *Letters of Queen Victoria* bear witness to the never-failing interest taken by the Queen in the army. Her sympathy with it took practical shape in the support of voluntary help for the troops in the Crimea, and in the personal presentation of medals to soldiers on their return from that country. She paid frequent visits to Aldershot and signed every military commission herself in three places. It has been recorded that, during the preparation of the troops in 1882 for the Tel-el-Kebir

[1] *Queen Victoria's Letters*, 1837–61, III, p. 372.

campaign, she addressed no fewer than seventeen notes
to the Secretary of State for War in a single day in August.
This attachment to the army endured throughout her long
reign, and it is well known that one of her last acts was to
interview Lord Roberts about the progress of the war in
South Africa within a week or two of her own death on
January 22nd, 1901.[1] The absence of plans for national
defence and military education were matters to which
she devoted considerable attention in conjunction with
the Commander-in-Chief and her ministers, to whom
numerous letters and memoranda were written explaining her views on what she thought would be to the benefit
of "her army".[2] At this time it was, perhaps, in the
question of the reconstitution of the army in India after
the Mutiny, that the Queen, as well as the Commander-
in-Chief, were mostly interested, in view of the great
importance of the decisions which had to be made. Was
the Secretary of State for India to have the powers exercised by the Secretary of State for War? Was the Commander-in-Chief to occupy the same position there as he
did at home? The Queen feared that her prerogatives in
army matters might be infringed if anything were done to
establish a British army in India independent of, and in
addition to, the regular army.[3] It was ultimately decided
to transfer some of the battalions which had been maintained by the East India Company, to the home army,
while the British force to be kept in India, and charged
against the annual budget of that country, was fixed at

[1] Lee, *Life of Queen Victoria*, pp. 247, 264, 329, 458, 538.
[2] *Queen Victoria's Letters*, 1837–61, III, pp. 269–70, 277–8, 280; *The Panmure Papers*, II, pp. 337–56.
[3] *Queen Victoria's Letters*, 1837–61, III, pp. 404, 410; *Disraeli's Life*, IV, p. 171.

eighty thousand of all ranks. A reorganisation of the native army was taken in hand at the same time. These changes were not completed until 1865, but the system of dual control by a Commander-in-Chief and the military member of the Governor-General's Council was not abolished until 1908, when Lord Kitchener was Commander-in-Chief and Lord Curzon, Viceroy.

The old objection to increasing the strength of the army had been based on the fear that the Crown would acquire too much power. In more modern days the principal obstacle to its enlargement was the question of its cost. Probably the burden of expense was always felt, but until 1860 it had not been strongly urged, although there were complaints of the weight of taxation, and arguments that more money could not be voted for the army. In 1857 Disraeli thought it inadvisable for England to become "a great military nation", but Palmerston argued that the army must at least be able to defend the country from attacks and insults.

"Nobody", he said, "dreams of England having a great standing army on the scale of the great nations of the Continent. But our army must be more than a domestic police. We have colonies to strengthen, possessions to maintain; and you must bear in mind that peace, however long it may continue, is not merely dependent on ourselves, but on the conduct of other Powers, and you must look forward to having a force sufficient at least to protect you in the outset from insult or attack. Depend upon it, for a country great and rich to leave itself without the means of defence is not a method to preserve peace in the long run."[1]

Before the Crimean War it was the fashion in some circles to imagine that an untrained and unorganised force, sup-

[1] *Disraeli's Life*, III, pp. 69–70; Martin, *Life of Prince Consort*, IV, p. 20 n.

ported by the patriotic spirit of its individual members, could be safely set the task of defeating an attack by thoroughly trained and highly organised continental troops. Government after government was faced but failed to cope with the urgent necessity of making Parliament consider in time of peace how best to prepare the country to meet the unhappy eventualities of war. One publication announced that if invasion did take place

the colliers of Northumberland could be whirled from the north to the south by the fuel that their sturdy hands have brought to the surface, and they alone would be a host to sweep the aggressor from our earth.[1]

However, the time was now approaching when the country was to witness a great transformation of its military organisation, in the course of which old customs and time-honoured institutions were to be replaced by a whole series of new methods and ideas. It was not the army alone that was affected by the activities of the politicians at Westminster. Disraeli, the chosen leader of the Tory party, made his contribution—"to dish the Whigs"—with the Reform Act of 1867, which enfranchised the borough householders, and abrogated the settlement effected by the Reform Bill of 1832. The Elementary Education Act of 1870 was passed, and competitive examinations were substituted for patronage as a means of entering the Civil Service. It was an age of reform, which had for its foundation a general demand for a greater efficiency in the public services.

The political situation abroad was not without its in-

[1] Charles Knight, *The Land We Live In*. Cf. C. J. Fox's speech in February, 1804, in which he advocated "an armed peasantry" as "the great defence of a country" against an invader, *Speeches*, VI, pp. 543-4.

fluence on the question of the future of the army. Little
had been done in the direction of improving its organisation since the tragic days of the Crimean War and Indian
Mutiny. Seventeen Royal Commissions, eighteen Select
Committees, nineteen Committees of Officers within the
War Office, besides thirty-five Committees of Military
Officers, had considered points of policy in a period of
twelve years.[1] Apparently it was hopeless to expect
definite progress to be made, so long as this country could
keep clear of wars on the larger scale. The spirit of indifference to military matters appeared to lull the nation
to sleep, as it had done so successfully after Waterloo.
There seemed to be no hope of lifting the army out of the
rut, and of giving it a form of government and organisation more in harmony with the requirements of the day.
However, the rapid rise of Prussia to a position of authority on the continent had created a profound impres-
sion, and much of her spectacular growth of power was
recognised as being directly attributable to her possession
of an army, maintained in a high state of efficiency. The
creation of this army may be said to date from her crushing defeat by Napoleon at Jena in 1806. It was after this
disaster that Scharnhorst and Stein took in hand the re-
building of the Prussian army, and succeeded in their
task in a manner which may well have been beyond their
fondest hopes. Despite the treaty of September, 1808,
they were able to train a larger body of men than Napoleon had intended to permit. They adopted a simple
process of passing the men into a reserve as soon as they
had received a modicum of military training, with the
liability of further service if and when they were recalled

[1] Clode, II, p. 394.

to the colours. This reserve gave the Prussian government an easy and efficacious manner of expanding the strength of its army, should the hour of need arise. It was a system that might well have been followed with advantage by this country, at any rate after 1815, but dependence on a reserve of ten thousand pensioners, who were allowed to serve at home in certain garrison towns, was preferred.

In 1866, in the Seven Weeks' War, the collapse of the Austrian army in the face of an attack by Prussia, proved that Bismarck had under his control a formidable military machine, ready to take the field, well organised and well equipped. That victorious campaign was followed by the crushing defeats inflicted on the French army in 1870-1, when the careful preparation and patient organisation of the German army in the preceding years had as much to do with the disastrous overthrow of France as the leadership of Von Moltke. The victories of Wörth and Spicheren, the investment of Metz, the surrender of the French Emperor at Sedan and the Siege of Paris came as a shock to this country, where many people had always considered the French army to be the greatest military force in Europe. This campaign, following on Prussia's successful operations in 1866, helped to stir the national conscience and to educate public opinion in this country to a realisation of the necessity of making continuous military preparations in peace, if the army were to be of any value in a war conducted under modern conditions. The day of improvisation in the face of the enemy was gone, and an army that could not take the field on the outbreak of war, provided with adequate reserves from which to make good the inevitable wastage in men, animals and equipment, was likely to find its prospects of success most gravely, if not irreparably prejudiced.

These events gave increased importance to the reforms in military organisation which were being carried out by the British government. At a general election which took place in November, 1868, the Liberal party was successful at the polls, and Gladstone became Prime Minister for the first time. Cardwell was appointed Secretary of State for War. He had held office in previous administrations as President of the Board of Trade, as Irish Secretary, and as Colonial Secretary, and thus had had considerable practical experience in the administration of public affairs before he went to the War Office. He was, it is said, Gladstone's ablest lieutenant, and has been called a "perfect administrator".[1] The Duke of Cambridge said that he was "a most gentlemanlike man, with whom it will be pleasant to act".[2] Early in December, 1868, he submitted a memorandum to Gladstone pointing out that the reorganisation, carried out at the time of the Crimean War, remained as the basis of our army organisation, without regard to the Committee of 1860, and that the system was still the same, without any principles to guide it. Under the arrangements made in 1861 the Secretary of State was responsible for finance, and the Commander-in-Chief for discipline.

"I contend", he wrote, "for the principle of plenary responsibility to Parliament on the part of the Parliamentary head of the Department; and, consequently, for the absence of all reservations express or implied from the authority of that officer."[3]

[1] Morley, *Life of Gladstone*, I, p. 746 (Popular ed.).
[2] Verner, I, p. 387.
[3] *Cardwell at the War Office*, p. 250.

In other words, he claimed full powers for the Secretary of State, a matter of difficulty in view of the known attitude of both the Sovereign and the Commander-in-Chief. He went on to enumerate various subjects for parliamentary discussion, such as the appointment and promotion of officers, including purchase; seniority, selection and education; recruiting, and the merits of long and short services; alteration of the numbers serving in the Colonies; consideration of short service in the army followed by service as reservists; inducements to officers and men in civil employment on retiring; and the maintenance and number of distinctions between the Guards and the Line.[1]

In March, 1862, in a debate in the House of Commons on imperial defence, a resolution had been carried urging that the Colonies, which enjoyed the rights of self-government, should undertake the main responsibility for providing the means for their own defence, while they could still claim imperial aid for their protection. This declaration of policy was the modern method of endeavouring to do what George Grenville had attempted in regard to the Colonies in North America before the War of Independence, when an effort had been made to establish the principle that America should make some contribution towards the cost of her own defence. Ireland had maintained a separate establishment prior to the Act of Union, but, despite the vulnerability of the Empire, no colonial forces had been organised elsewhere on a serious basis. However, by the time that Cardwell introduced his first estimates on March 9th, 1869, in which he gave an exposition of British military policy as he

[1] *Cardwell at the War Office*, pp. 253-4.

viewed it, the situation had changed. The first of the main points to which he drew attention was that since 1868 the self-governing Colonies had become partly responsible for their own measures of defence, in virtue of the establishment of local militia and volunteers. The consequence of this development was to make possible the reduction of the garrisons scattered all over the world, thereby expanding the forces at home, with a concurrent decrease in expenditure and an increase in efficiency. The second point was that the advent of the steamship as a means of carrying out movements of troops had affected our strategic conceptions. There was no need to keep our forces dispersed in small garrisons in every direction as troops could be taken by steamship to any threatened point. The striking force should be at home, concentrated and ready to move when and where required. This concentration opened the way to a reduction in the regular forces, but the militia was increased as a reserve for the army, while the number of volunteers was also augmented.

Lord Northbrook, who later went to India as Viceroy after the murder of Lord Mayo in 1872, was Cardwell's Parliamentary Under-Secretary of State, and presided over a Committee which was formed in 1868 to enquire into the existing arrangements for conducting War Office business. This Committee issued a series of important reports, the first of which, dealing with financial supervision, was published a few days after Cardwell had introduced the estimates of 1869. It began by describing the whole situation, the division of responsibility, and the lack of consultation between the War Office and the Horse Guards. The Committee reported that a more perfect theory of administrative organisation lay in the union of finance and administration, so that financial considerations might attend on administrative policy from its inception, as well as control it during its progress, and review it in anticipation of each financial year.[1]

The two considerations of how much to spend, and of how much ought to be spent, naturally influence each other and require consideration by one brain. Cardwell could think in terms of finance as well as of military policy. He saw the Empire's strategic problems as a whole, affecting both the navy and the army. He cut down expenditure, but conceived a short-service army with a system of rapid expansion in time of war.

The Committee reviewed the relative positions of the War Office and the Horse Guards. In 1854 when various departments were placed under the Secretary of State, the Horse Guards remained independent. After the Crimean War, the name "War Office" took the place of "War Department", and the offices of the Deputy-Secretary at War and of the Clerk of the Ordnance were abolished, the duties of both being merged in the office of an Under-Secretary of State. This system was defective because there was no grouping of departments giving an intermediate authority between the Secretary of State or the Under-Secretary. They were each directly responsible for a large number of departments working independently, instead of the whole organisation being closely knit together under the superintendence of one person. The Northbrook Committee recommended that the War Office should be divided into the following three departments: (1) the Commander-in-Chief, who was to be the sole

---

[1] *Cardwell at the War Office*, p. 20.

military adviser of the Secretary of State and in charge of the regular army and the auxiliary forces; (2) the Surveyor-General of Ordnance, who was to be responsible for supply, transport, clothing and munitions of war, including the purchase, construction and charge of *matériel*; and (3) the Financial Secretary, who was to control all the financial business of the army, including the audit of accounts and the handling of the estimates submitted by the Secretary of State to Parliament. The Committee considered that it was essential for the Commander-in-Chief to be under the same roof as the Secretary of State.

"Indeed," the report stated, "as a practical question, no scheme which is not based upon the accomplished fact that all the departments of military administration are housed under the same roof can be otherwise than abortive."

The Committee of 1860 had made a similar recommendation, and General Jonathan Peel, a former Secretary of State for War, had stated in evidence that, apart from the convenience and advantage to the service of having both offices in the same building, the separation engendered the belief that they were distinct departments, and this idea in turn tended to "antagonism on the part of military men against the supremacy of the civil power".[1]

The Duke of Cambridge was strongly opposed to the suggestion, considering that the prestige of the Commander-in-Chief would be lowered if his office were removed from Whitehall to Pall Mall. He wrote:

The removal of the Commander-in-Chief to the office at Pall Mall, deprived, as he must be, moreover, of all his military

[1] Minutes of Evidence 3789-3790, *Report*, 1860.

surroundings, would place him in a position of subordination which would virtually deprive him of all his specific attributes and would in fact place him more or less on an equality with the Controller-in-Chief, or any one of the Under-Secretaries of State. This would be a degeneration which would altogether alter his status in the estimation of the army and the public, and would, in my opinion, be most injurious to the interests of the Crown, the real head of the army, and also to the public service.[1]

The Queen had written to Mr Cardwell in the same strain, stating that "such a step could not fail to damage the position of the Commander-in-Chief", her argument being based on the theory that the army was directly controlled by the Crown.[2] The Secretary of State was in favour of the recommendation, and in explaining to the House of Commons his scheme of dividing the War Office into the three departments as proposed by the Northbrook Committee, said that it was essential for the War Office and the Horse Guards to be under one roof to stop friction and suspicion. For the moment it was impracticable to carry it out, so he had begun by forbidding correspondence between the departments. That step, in 1869, had reduced the number of letters by thirty thousand in the two departments. Personal interchange of information had taken the place of minutes.[3] The Committee's recommendations were adopted, and the War Office was divided into the three departments of the Commander-in-Chief, the Surveyor-General of Ordnance, and the Financial Secretary, who might each be in

[1] Verner, I, 409.
[2] *Queen Victoria's Letters*, 1862–78, I, pp. 584–5; Lee, *Life of Queen Victoria*, p. 409.
[3] *Cardwell at the War Office*, pp. 54–55.

Parliament.[1] The Duke of Cambridge was given a room at the War Office, whence he wrote his letters under the address "Horse Guards, Pall Mall". The Secretary of State became responsible for army business as a whole by the War Office Act of 1870, and his duties were defined in an Order-in-Council of June 4th of that year. The same order placed the Commander-in-Chief in a position of complete subordination to the political head of the department. The Queen thus agreed to a proposal to which she had taken exception in 1860 as an attempt to diminish the royal prerogative of controlling the army without interference from Parliament or its representatives. From this time onward, the "costly and inefficient" system of dual control came to an end, and the major question of the future was how to evolve a workable organisation at the War Office in place of what Florence Nightingale once described as

a very slow office, an enormously expensive office, a not very efficient office, and one in which the minister's intentions can be entirely negatived by all his sub-departments and those of each of the sub-departments by every other.[2]

It is doubtful if the Queen and the Commander-in-Chief really understood the necessity of a complete overhaul of army headquarters organisation. The ministers wished to abolish the inconvenience of the situation arising from the fact that there were two separate offices, which had to work in the closest possible touch with each other if army business was to be run with the maximum degree of

---

[1] War Office Act, 33–34 Vict. c. 17 and Order-in-Council June 4th, 1870.
[2] *Cardwell at the War Office*, pp. 238–40; Gwynn and Tuckwell, *Life of Sir Charles Dilke*, I, pp. 77, 137–8; Lee, *Life of Queen Victoria*, p. 409; Stanmore, *Memoirs of Sidney Herbert*, II, p. 369.

efficiency combined with the minimum amount of expenditure. The Duke had been in office for about twelve years and did not favour alterations. He said, in the House of Lords, that he felt that the proposed amalgamation of departments, and his subordination to the Secretary of State, destroyed all that he valued in the army.

The establishment of a Surveyor-General of Ordnance at the War Office can be traced to a Committee, under the chairmanship of Lord Strathnairn, which was appointed in 1866 to consider the transport duties of the army in the field. A few weeks after its appointment, Lord John Russell's government fell. General Peel, who was Secretary of State for War in the new Cabinet formed by Lord Derby, directed the Committee to extend its enquiries into the administration of the supply departments of the army. Far-reaching investigations were conducted, and the Committee's report contained proposals on the formation of the "department of control" to deal with all the supply services. On the recommendation of the Northbrook Committee, Cardwell adopted the scheme as a whole. He appointed a Surveyor-General of Ordnance, who was to be the head of the "Control Department". He was to be a military officer of high rank and could occupy a seat in Parliament. The title, "Control Department", created suspicion at once in the army, and the scheme miscarried. The intention had been to assist and interest General Officers in the details of the business side of army administration, but it was not unnaturally supposed that the idea was to control and check them in the course of their normal duties. The result was that the Conservative government, that came into office in 1874, abolished the system, replacing it by two new departments—the Commissariat and Transport Department, and the Ordnance Stores Department, both under the Commander-in-Chief in camps and garrison towns. At the War Office, they still remained under the Surveyor-General and the Financial Secretary.

Prior to 1857, the Commander-in-Chief had been the adviser of the Secretary of State on all military questions. In that year an officer was appointed Secretary for Military Correspondence in the Secretary of State's office, a post which subsequently developed into that of Permanent Under-Secretary of War.[1] He had the right of direct access to the Secretary of State. Before long complaints were made that the advice of the Commander-in-Chief was ignored, and that the answers to questions submitted by him to the government were those of subordinate military officers. The position was reviewed in the third report of Lord Northbrook's Committee, which recommended the reconstitution of the Military Secretary's office under the Commander-in-Chief with a civilian as Under-Secretary for War. It was held that the Military Secretary's duties should be confined to the promotion and appointment of officers; that he should cease to be the personal staff officer of the Commander-in-Chief; and that he should hold his appointment for five years on the same basis as other staff officers such as the Adjutant-General. Cardwell was anxious to give effect to these proposals so that the selection of officers might be submitted to him and the Commander-in-Chief by a responsible military officer. A lengthy discussion arose on the question. The Queen did not like the proposed reorganisation thinking that it would mean that the Military

[1] *The Panmure Papers*, ii, pp. 343–4.

Secretary would be independent of the Commander-in-Chief, whose position would be undermined, as the Secretary of State would consult the Military Secretary without reference to the Commander-in-Chief. Cardwell pointed out that the Commander-in-Chief's powers in selection would be increased by the suggested alternative, and that the Secretary of State would have to defend the Commander-in-Chief's choice in Parliament, whenever that choice was questioned. He assured the Queen that Parliament would not approve of vesting extensive powers of selection in the Commander-in-Chief. The Queen was not persuaded by these arguments, saying that she would not sanction the arrangements unless the Secretary of State and the Commander-in-Chief came to an agreement. Cardwell assured her that he wished to uphold the position of the Commander-in-Chief, and "to preserve the army's confidence that the patronage of the army is not disposed of...for the convenience of a political party".[1] After considerable discussion, it was finally agreed that the Military Secretary was to be selected by the Commander-in-Chief with the approval of the Secretary of State. He was to be as subordinate as the Adjutant-General and to hold office for five years.

The idea underlying these suggested reforms was to make the Secretary of State responsible to Parliament for all military business, and to give him complete control over the whole administration of the army in the closest possible co-operation with the Commander-in-Chief. He would have as much responsibility for questions of discipline and promotion, as for matters arising on

[1] *Queen Victoria's Letters*, 1862–78, II, pp. 112–19.

financial policy. The Commander-in-Chief would be the principal military adviser. It was thought that if the situation was so clearly defined that the supremacy of the Secretary of State was indisputable, the jealousy of the War Office then felt by so many military officers would tend to diminish or disappear altogether. It was not intended that the Secretary of State should interfere in the daily routine of discipline, but he would be definitely responsible to Parliament for all the actions of the Commander-in-Chief. This view of the situation was in accord with the working practice of the constitutional system of the country, under which all acts of administration are the definite responsibility of some parliamentary officer. It was agreed on all hands that it was a matter of primary importance to keep the Commander-in-Chief free from all danger of political pressure, so that the Secretary of State could defend him from the difficulties arising out of personal appeals from members of either of the Houses of Parliament. It was considered that the service as a whole would benefit if the Commander-in-Chief were "brought more into council in the War Office", and would learn to think less that that department was administered almost entirely by civilians. It was felt that the time had come to move in the direction of bringing about a real co-ordination of the work of the two offices, which had remained too long almost distinct and, certainly, aloof from each other, although they both existed in theory and in practice to serve a common object.

In 1867 a Royal Commission on recruiting, presided over by Lord Dalhousie, who as Lord Panmure had been Secretary of State for War during the Crimean War, reported. From 1858 to 1870, the army lived a hand-to-mouth existence; it was mostly abroad; colour service was for life. An attempt to form a reserve had failed, as the number of reservists stood at just over three thousand men. The latter was the weakest link in the chain, and Cardwell had to find a remedy which would place the army on a basis to enable it to meet the requirements of modern warfare. The Army Enlistment Act of 1870 established an important principle, which has remained ever since as a part of the foundations upon which the whole edifice of the modern British army has been erected. It gave statutory approval to the argument that the regular army in peace should form a nucleus to be joined by reservists on the outbreak of war. The Prussian victories over Austria in 1866 had shown how formidable an army composed of soldiers who had spent two or three years in the ranks could be, and how great was the value of a system which enabled the peace army to be strengthened by recalling to its ranks numbers of men who had only completed their active military training a comparatively short time before. Cardwell was convinced of the soundness of those views, and recognised how greatly our military strength suffered from the complete lack of any adequate reserve upon which the serving army could depend for reinforcements in times of emergency. He therefore introduced by this Act of Parliament the modern system of short service with the colours, followed by a period in the reserve, which provided the army with a professional reserve of trained men, who could be recalled for service at any moment. He met with some opposition from the school whose theory was that the best soldiers were those who spent the greater part of their lives in the army. At the same time, the evil system of bounties was abolished, while the enlistment of criminals was forbidden, and the discharge of men of bad character was authorised.

The Army Regulation Bill of the following year proposed the abolition of the system of purchase of commissions. The Queen had agreed to the proposal, and had informed the Secretary of State that she could say nothing against it if the government were prepared to deal generously with the officers.[1] It was an old subject, and the question had been discussed at frequent intervals in Parliament. Attempts had been made from time to time to regulate the position, but they had not met with success. For instance, in 1809, an Act of Parliament prohibited over-regulation prices being paid on pain of "forfeit of commission and being cashiered".[2] The result was, that an officer who retired got the regulation price from the government, while his successor paid the over-regulation price to him. This method of obtaining officers was supported by the Duke of Wellington who said that British officers were

from education, manners, and habits, the best officers in the world, and that to compose the officers of a lower class would cause the army to deteriorate,

and that

promotion by purchase exempts the British army from the character of a mercenary army.

Lord Palmerston was of the same opinion, holding that

it was only when the army was unconnected with those whose property gave them an interest in the welfare of the country,

[1] Queen Victoria's Letters, 1862–78, II, pp. 114–15.
[2] 49 Geo. III, c. 126. The over-regulation price was the price paid in excess of the price allowed by the tariff drawn up by government.

and was commanded by unprincipled adventurers, that it would ever become formidable to the liberties of the nation.

Apparently, it was the idea that the safety of the country and the maintenance of the constitution were bound up with the purchase system. On the other hand, there had been annual motions in the House of Commons for its abolition. Herbert had investigated the question but encountered strong opposition from many quarters including the Queen, the Prince Consort, the Commander-in-Chief, and even from Lord Panmure and Lord Grey, who were both known to be zealous supporters of army reform in other directions. The strongest opposition, however, came from the Prince Consort, who foresaw that the abolition of purchase involved the ultimate control of promotion and military appointments by the Secretary of State, the representative of Parliament, and not by the Commander-in-Chief, the representative of the Crown. As a result, nothing further was done by Herbert, and it was left to Cardwell to bring the question to the front again.[1] The Commander-in-Chief was still opposed to the change, considering that the existing plan had worked favourably for the army, and kept the officers young and gentlemen. This objection did not meet the point that the system had not helped to produce an efficient army, an important argument in view of what had happened in the Franco-Prussian War. The bill proposed to abolish purchase, but officers leaving the army were to have the over-regulation prices paid to them, at an estimated cost to the country of about £7,000,000. It passed the House of Commons without any serious difficulty, despite the opposition of certain Conservative

[1] Stanmore, *Memoirs of Sidney Herbert*, II, pp. 373-5.

members, who talked about "a sop to democracy" and "a professional army". It was said that the "Horse Guards" was opposed to the change. Cardwell told the House of Commons it was "necessary for the Commander-in-Chief to be in harmony with the government of the day", while the Prime Minister said, with the Queen's approval, that the military arrangements of the government of the day must ever have the energetic co-operation of the chiefs of the army.

When the bill reached the House of Lords, the Duke of Richmond moved an amendment, declaring that that House was unwilling to agree to the motion until a comprehensive and complete scheme of army reorganisation was laid before it. This amendment was carried by a majority of twenty-five on July 17th. The Cabinet met on the following day, and Gladstone advised the Queen to cancel the warrant under which purchase was legal. This advice was embodied in a formal Cabinet minute, and a Royal Warrant to give effect to it was signed by the Queen on the 20th of the month. It was an exercise of the executive power against the constitutional power, which the Attorney-General, Sir Roundell Palmer, supported, by stating that such a warrant "was within the undoubted power of the Crown".[1] The House of Lords expressed its displeasure, by censuring the government for its action. It may be added that the abolition of purchase entailed the introduction of pensions for officers at the expense of the State.

The position between the Commander-in-Chief and the Secretary of State had not been improved by the

[1] *Cardwell at the War Office*, p. 259; Morley, *Life of Gladstone*, I, pp. 747–51; *Queen Victoria's Letters*, 1862–78, II, pp. 141–54.

course of events. The former was a member of the House of Lords and accustomed to take part in debates on military questions. So long as he was in agreement with the political head of the army, it did not matter, but in the case of a difference of opinion, it was difficult to adjust the situation. Cardwell told the Duke that he must either resign or support him. The Duke replied that he must say what he felt in Parliament, and must say what he felt as a technical adviser. A compromise was arranged on the purchase question, and the Commander-in-Chief supported the government in a speech in the House of Lords when he learnt that the House of Commons was prepared to treat officers liberally.[1] The possibility of the Secretary of State, and the chief military adviser of the government taking diametrically opposite views on the same questions in Parliament, illustrated with unmistakable clearness the danger of having two masters in one house. It was a source of undoubted weakness in organisation. The personal characteristics and temperaments of the principal actors were important factors, and played a considerable part in the events of the next few years, when the administration of the War Office was no bed of roses, with the fierce glare of the searchlight of public enquiry constantly playing upon all its doings.

The Army Regulation Bill, in which the abolition of purchase had been originally brought before Parliament, also contained proposals for the resumption by the Crown of its direct authority over the militia, yeomanry and volunteers. It was considered that the time had come to abolish the system of the local control of the militia by the Lords-Lieutenant, and that that force should be put under

<hr />

[1] Verner, II, pp. 20–6.

the War Office, the officers being granted commissions by the Queen. It was part of Cardwell's general plan to raise the military efficiency of the auxiliary forces, which he hoped might gradually become an effective part of the military resources of the country. The Lords-Lieutenant regained their connection with the local forces when the Territorial Force was established in 1907 as part of the Haldane scheme for the reorganisation of the army. Lastly, powers were obtained under which the government could take possession of any railway in the United Kingdom in the event of a national emergency.

CHAPTER V

IN 1873, as a result of a ministerial crisis, Gladstone became Chancellor of the Exchequer as well as First Lord of the Treasury. He demanded reductions in the naval and military estimates for the next financial year, but Goschen and Cardwell as the ministers responsible for the two services, were unable to agree with his proposals. The deadlock thus produced was suddenly brought to an end by Gladstone's announcement of a dissolution in January, 1874.[1] The Conservative party, led by Disraeli, who had picturesquely described the Liberal ministers in a speech at Manchester nearly two years before as "a range of exhausted volcanoes", won a substantial victory at the ensuing general election. Gladstone resigned office and was succeeded by Disraeli as Prime Minister. The major pre-occupation of the new government in the six years between 1874 and 1880 lay in the field of international affairs, while the army enjoyed what Lord Wolseley called "six years of peace". It is possible that the interest in military matters aroused by the events of 1866 and 1870–1 had already begun to wane, and that the old spirit of apathy and neglect of military matters was

[1] *Queen Victoria's Letters*, 1862–78, II, p. 305; *Life of Gladstone*, VI, ch. xiv; *Disraeli's Life*, v, ch. viii.

beginning to reassert itself in contrast to the reforming activities introduced during Lord Cardwell's regime at the War Office. The hope of educating the public to take and maintain anything more than the most fleeting interest in the crucial question of defence during a period when this country's relations with foreign powers in Europe were undisturbed by any actual hostilities, was never great. During the next thirty years, the small band of military reformers despaired of seeing the introduction of what they would have considered a sound system of army administration. It is probably true that time was required in which to digest some of the more recently introduced alterations, and that the wave of political opinion which had borne the Conservative party into power was the electorate's method of declaring that a halt should be called to the process of carrying out political and social as well as military reforms.

However, certain details of the Cardwell system remained to be further developed if the beneficial results of what had been accomplished already were not to be lost, and it was in this direction that the new government proceeded. In 1872-3 Cardwell had produced the localisation scheme. Brigade districts were created with consecutive numbers in which regular battalions were linked in pairs. Two militia battalions were affiliated to these linked battalions, the whole forming a brigade district with a brigade depot behind it. In 1876, Gathorne-Hardy, who was Secretary of State for War in Disraeli's government, appointed a Committee under Colonel Stanley to consider the militia and brigade depot system. This Committee recommended that the two line and the two militia battalions should form a territorial regiment with the same name and the same depot. They were to form one complete unit, the regular battalions being the first and second battalions, while the third and fourth battalions were to be created from the existing militia battalions. The depot, which was common to all, was to be the last battalion of the series. The Queen and the Commander-in-Chief disliked this extension of the Cardwell scheme. The report of the Stanley Committee was "distasteful" to the latter.

"I have heard", the Duke of Cambridge declared, "a good deal of localising the Army but the man who urges that does not know what he is talking about. The Army of England could not be localised. A great portion of it has to be abroad."[1]

In 1879 Lord Airey presided over a Committee which was set up to enquire into certain defects in the short service system and the localisation scheme. The Committee were informed that there was "no intention on the part of the Government to depart from the general principles of reorganisation which had been accepted by the country since 1870", and the "formation of the army in regiments of more than one battalion for the purposes of mutual support" was given as one of the general principles. By the time that the Committee reported, Childers had become Secretary of State for War in the Liberal government which came into office in 1880. He disagreed with the Committee's recommendation that the unlinking of battalions and the creation of large depots were means of improving the short service system. He held that, if the Cardwell system was to be carried out, it must be developed to the fullest possible extent. The Committee's proposals were not adopted by the govern-

[1] Verner, II, p. 204.

ment. The territorial system proposed by Colonel Stanley's Committee was introduced in the Regulation of the Forces Act passed in 1881, under which the linked battalions lost their numbers and were formed into regiments of two battalions, regimental districts taking the place of brigade districts.[1]

As a result of the General Election in the spring of 1880, the Liberal party had secured a majority in the House of Commons, and after the Queen had unsuccessfully approached both Lord Hartington and Lord Granville, Gladstone was called upon to form a ministry and sent Childers to the War Office with Campbell-Bannerman, a future Secretary of State for War, as his Financial Secretary.

The new administration did not enter upon a large programme of military reform, and was content to leave the organisation of the army more or less as it found it. Reference may be made here to one or two other matters of interest which occurred at this time. After the new government took office, the Duke of Cambridge addressed a letter to the Secretary of State in which he re-defined his position.

"The command of the army", he wrote, "rests with the Commander-in-Chief, as representing the Sovereign; the Secretary of State is the high political official who controls all army matters and represents the Department, for which he is fully responsible to Parliament. But he certainly does not command the army...the command-in-chief cannot be merged in the Secretary of State under present conditions, and my position must have an individuality, which it is essential and necessary to maintain."[2]

[1] General Order of 1881.
[2] Childers, *Life*, II, pp. 55–7.

This reiteration of his views was in the nature of a challenge to the opinions which were gradually becoming common to all political parties, and it was felt that an answer was required. Childers, a supporter of the policy of the supremacy of the parliamentary officer in the shape of the Secretary of State for War, referred to the question in a speech to his constituents at Pontefract on January 19th, 1882. He explained his view of the position of both Secretary of State and Commander-in-Chief and contested the view that the Crown still governed the army. He said:

> It has been suggested that of late years successive Secretaries of State have, in the government of the army, been encroaching on the functions of others. The army, these critics say, is the army of the Crown; we, Secretaries of State forsooth, want to make it the army of the House of Commons. The Crown, they say, governs the army through the Commander-in-Chief. The Secretary of State is a mere financial officer, who has gradually intruded on the province of the Crown by means of the power of the purse.

He pointed out that the Queen, who was the most constitutional of Sovereigns, was the head of the army as of every other branch of the public service. She could do no wrong because her acts were the acts of her advisers, that is, of her responsible ministers. The question of the Secretary of State for War was not a matter of custom, nor of unwritten law. His functions were laid down by the Order of the Queen in Council of June, 1870, as "administering the Royal Authority and Prerogative in respect of the Army". Under him, there were three great departments, each equally responsible to him. They were the Commander-in-Chief for the Military Department;

the Surveyor-General for the Ordnance and Supply Department; and the Financial Secretary for the Finance Department. No action, no appointment, no movement, and no payment could be made without the authority of the Secretary of State.

"To say", he declared, "that the Secretary of State has no controlling power in such matters, when he is responsible to Parliament for any improper exercise of the Queen's prerogative in regard to them, is manifestly absurd. On this subject I have never known any misapprehension within the walls of the War Office or in Parliament."[1]

This statement clearly laid down the position of the Secretary of State as the constitutional authority in relation to the Commander-in-Chief. As the responsible minister of the Crown, the Secretary of State was bound to assert the authority which he derived from his office as one of Her Majesty's principal Secretaries of State. He had to bear the ultimate responsibility for everything done in connection with the army, and to be ready to explain, defend and justify the actions of the Commander-in-Chief as fully as those of anybody else employed with or in the military forces of the Crown. It was a task which could not be shared with anybody, and the last word, the final decision, had to lie with the minister who was answerable to Parliament.

In 1882, the high expectations of those who had pressed for the introduction of the short-service army as a fundamental portion of the country's military organisation, were fully justified by the success which attended the calling-up of the reserves for the first time on the occasion of the war in Egypt after Arabi Pasha's revolt. A year

[1] Childers, *Life*, II, pp. 55-7.

later, a change of importance was introduced when the Commissariat Department was placed under the control of the Commander-in-Chief and became a purely military body. The Ordnance and Pay Departments followed, with the result that, outside the War Office, civil control of these departments came to an end. The failure of certain items of equipment issued to the troops in the Nile campaign of 1884–5 led to the consideration of the advisability of transferring the duties of the Surveyor-General and the Director of Supplies and Transport to the Commander-in-Chief, the theory being that responsibility for the efficiency of the army could not be placed upon the military authorities unless they were granted full powers in regard to equipment, food, transport and other services. It was considered that they alone could know what was most suitable for the army and were in the best position to secure what was required. Accordingly, it was argued, the position of the Commander-in-Chief should be strengthened by the transfer of all army services to his side of the War Office. He would then be responsible in reality for the whole military machine, and no longer in the irksome position of sharing his responsibilities with a civil branch, whose knowledge of the army's requirements was largely theoretical.

The decision to give effect to this proposal was made by Lord Salisbury's government which came into office after the Home Rule Election of 1886. Stanhope, who had become Secretary of State for War when Lord Randolph Churchill resigned the Chancellorship of the Exchequer towards the end of that year on the grounds that he was not supported by his colleagues in the Cabinet in a policy of financial retrenchment, abolished the Surveyor-

General's office.[1] It had been a political appointment held by a member of Parliament since 1875. This step involved the transfer of the administrative control of army services from civilian to military hands at the War Office, thus placing the headquarters arrangements on the same footing as those which had existed in camps and garrisons since 1875 when the Control Department was abandoned.

Under a second Order-in-Council, War Office business was distributed between a military and a civil division, both under the administrative control of the Secretary of State.[2] The Commander-in-Chief became responsible to the parliamentary head of the department for everything connected with the efficiency of the soldier—discipline, training, housing, clothing, food and armament. On the civil side, the Financial Secretary was charged with expenditure, account and audit, payment of money, and the control of the manufacturing departments. This system remained in force until the Duke of Cambridge retired in 1895. At first the changes were generally welcomed, but, in the course of time, they had to run the gauntlet of a considerable volume of hostile criticism, because the considered opinion of competent observers was that the burden placed upon the shoulders of the Commander-in-Chief was greater than he could bear.

In the summer of 1889, the government appointed a fresh Royal Commission to investigate the administration of the War Office as so many other commissions and committees had already done. It is not without interest to note the circumstances which led to its appointment.

[1] Order-in-Council dated December 29th, 1887.
[2] Order-in-Council dated February 21st, 1888.

The condition of both the army and the navy had become a source of grave anxiety by 1887. Gladstone's government of 1880 and the administration headed by Lord Salisbury, which came into office in 1886, had exhibited considerable weakness in handling army reforms. The latter told the Queen there was no army capable of meeting even a second-class continental power.[1] There was waste and inefficiency. The cost of the land services between 1875 and 1887 rose by £4,000,000, and the increase between 1870 and 1887 amounted to nearly £9,000,000.[2] The Queen realised that reforms were required in the land service, but she did not understand how difficult it was to make changes in face of the resistance offered by the Duke of Cambridge. As far back as 1879 Disraeli, in a letter to Lady Bradford, had written:

> The Horse Guards will ruin this country, unless there is a Prime Minister who will have his way, and that cannot be counted upon. Fortunately he has the power, if he only had the determination. You cannot get a Secretary of War to resist the cousin of the Sovereign, with whom he is placed in daily and hourly communication. I tremble when I think what may be the fate of this country if, as is not unlikely, a great struggle occur, with the Duke of Cambridge's generals.[3]

Lord Wolseley wrote in despair to the Queen from Korti in March, 1885, saying that

> no government, Whig or Tory, has the honesty to tell the people the truth and take them into their confidence on Army and Navy matters.[4]

---

[1] *Queen Victoria's Letters*, 1886–1901, I, pp. 194–5.
[2] Churchill, *Life of Lord Randolph Churchill*, II, pp. 316, 320.
[3] *Disraeli's Life*, VI, pp. 473–4.
[4] *Queen Victoria's Letters*, 1879–85, III, pp. 630–2.

In 1887, a Commission on army administration over which Sir James Stephen had presided, reported that it was morally and physically impossible for any man to discharge satisfactorily the duties which fell to the Secretary of State for War. No steps were taken to put matters on a proper foundation. Expenditure tended to increase without any assurance that an adequate return in the shape of greater efficiency was being secured. The War Office could not mobilise an army corps. The militia was weak in officers. The volunteer corps were short of guns.

These questions came to a head when Lord Charles Beresford resigned from the Board of Admiralty at the beginning of 1888, because he could do nothing to remedy the state of affairs existing in the navy, where he alleged there was a lack of systematic preparation for war. In May of that year, Lord Wolseley made a grave statement in the House of Lords on the position of the country's military arrangements which, he stated, were not organised nor equipped as they should be to guarantee the safety of the metropolis.[1] The immediate results were to be seen in the passing of certain Acts of Parliament on defence questions, and the remission of the consideration of the whole problem to the new Royal Commission over which Lord Hartington agreed to preside.[2] The terms of reference were:

To inquire into the civil and professional administration of the Naval and Military Departments, and the relation of those Departments to each other and to the Treasury; and to report what changes in their existing system would tend to the efficiency and economy of the public service.

[1] *Wolseley's Life*, p. 240.
[2] The correspondence in *Queen Victoria's Letters*, 1886–90, I, throws much interesting light on this subject.

The other members of the Committee were Lord Randolph Churchill, the Right Hon. W. H. Smith, the Right Hon. Henry Campbell-Bannerman, Sir Richard Temple, Admiral Richards, General Brackenbury, and Mr Ismay. The evidence given before this body was suppressed "because the differences of opinion in high quarters were so acute as to render publication indiscreet".[1]

The first report issued by the Commission in May, 1889, was mainly concerned with the relations of the Admiralty and the War Office. It suggested, tentatively, the creation of a Naval and Military Council under the chairmanship of the Prime Minister, comprising the First Lord of the Admiralty and the Secretary of State for War with their principal professional advisers, to ensure co-operation between the two departments upon whose decisions in the event of war the whole safety of the Empire might well depend.

The second report, which appeared in the following year, reviewed the internal administration of the War Office. The Commission stated that

the complete responsibility, to Parliament and the Country, of the Secretary of State for the discipline as well as for the administration of the army, must now be accepted as definitely established.[2]

In theory, his constitutional responsibility was already complete, but, in practice, the fact that the Commander-in-Chief approached the Sovereign direct tended to diminish it. No definite opinion was expressed on the working of the new scheme "so recently inaugurated and to some extent incompletely developed" by Mr Stan-

[1] *Wolseley's Life*, p. 241.   [2] *Report*, para. 82, c. 5979, 1890.

hope, but it was considered that there was too great a burden on the shoulders of the Commander-in-Chief, who was the only military officer responsible to the Secretary of State.

"Under the present system", the Commissioners remarked, "the only real responsibility appears to rest on the Commander-in-Chief, who alone would be accountable to the Secretary of State, even for such a matter as the defective design of a heavy gun. We do not find this centralisation of responsibility exists in the administration of the armies of any of the Great Powers of Europe, and we consider that it cannot conduce to efficiency."

It was held that the existing scheme failed to make the heads of the different departments responsible to the Secretary of State, and did not provide him with a satisfactory system of obtaining independent advice. The members of the Commission considered that no future Commander-in-Chief could manage as the Duke of Cambridge had done, but that there was a lack of consultation between the various branches at the War Office. Suggestions were made which it was thought might be carried out when a suitable opportunity arose. These recommendations included the abolition of the post of Commander-in-Chief, the appointment of a General Officer Commanding in Great Britain, and of a Chief of Staff. It was further proposed to throw definite responsibilities on the heads of the various departments, who would be individually answerable to the Secretary of State for their administrative work, and advise him collectively as a permanent War Office Council. The military members of this body were to be the Chief of the Staff, the Adjutant-General, the Quartermaster-General, the Director of Artillery, and the Inspector-General of Fortifications, with the Secretary of State, the Parliamentary Under-Secretary, the Permanent Under-Secretary, and the Permanent Financial Secretary, as civilian members.

The General Officer Commanding in Great Britain was to be responsible for the command and inspection of the troops stationed at home, and was to be employed outside the War Office. The Chief of the Staff was to be free from executive work, and his duties were described as follows:

(1) To advise the Secretary of State on military policy and as to the strength of the military forces.

(2) To collect and co-ordinate military information.

(3) To propose schemes for defence of the Empire and to prepare plans of action.

(4) To communicate with First Sea Lord on inter-departmental policy; to correspond with heads of other departments and with the General Officer Commanding in Great Britain on military policy.

(5) To report annually to the Secretary of State on the needs of the Empire.

Shortly, the proposals of the Commission were that the War Office should be remodelled on the lines of the Board of Admiralty which had been governed by an Act of Parliament passed in 1832.[1] The Secretary of State was to occupy a position analogous to that of the First Lord of the Admiralty, while the Chief of Staff would correspond to the First Naval Lord, and would be the most important of the military officers.

[1] 2 and 3 Will. IV, c. 40.

The proposals of the Commission aroused considerable opposition which centred round the suggested abolition of the post of Commander-in-Chief. Lord Hartington summed up the reasons for this recommendation in the course of a speech which he delivered in July, 1890. He said:

We have felt that, under our Constitution, it is impossible to place any direct control over the army, over army organisation, in the hands of any man except one who shall be directly responsible to the House of Commons. That being so, the question is narrowed to this; whether it is desirable to place between the parliamentary Chief and the heads of the various Departments into which the office must be divided, one great military officer, to whom all other departmental officers should be subordinate, and in whom all the lines of administration shall centre. In my opinion that is not a desirable link in the chain of War Office administration. I think that the existence of such an officer tends to weaken the sense of responsibility of each of the officers at the head of the Departments. It also tends to diminish the efficiency of the War Office Council. I do not think it possible, if you have an officer of the weight and influence of the Commander-in-Chief, however much you may modify his functions, that you will have that freedom of discussion in the War Office Council which will alone enable a civilian Minister adequately to decide, rightly and justly, the question of War Office administration.[1]

The difficulties of what Lord Hartington described as "giving the professional men more power and at the same time more responsibility" in conjunction with the existing parliamentary system were great indeed.[2] Many members of the public and of the army did not wish to

[1] Holland, *Life of the Duke of Devonshire*, II, pp. 219–20.
[2] *Life of Lord Randolph Churchill*, II, p. 323.

see the Commander-in-Chief disappear from his post at
the head of the service for which he had worked so long.
Their opposition to the proposal was as nothing to the
anger and dismay it caused in the highest circles. The
Queen said that it could not be allowed for one moment.
She wrote of "this really abominable report", and was
shocked beyond measure that it emanated from a Conservative government. She wished to see how "the reck-
less changes and incredibly thoughtless proposals can best
be met". She laid down various points such as the
necessity of the army remaining in direct communication
with the Sovereign through the Commander-in-Chief,
who must have the dispensation of patronage, subject to
the assent of the Secretary of State; the Chief of Staff to
be under and attached to the Commander-in-Chief, and
not to the Secretary of State; useful changes could be
made to facilitate communication, but they were hardly
necessary, as the Commander-in-Chief said there were
no difficulties; and, finally, "the Queen must consider her
successors and hand down her Crown unimpaired".[1] The
Duke of Cambridge wrote about saving "the Crown and
the Army from CATASTROPHE that must befall them" if
the post of Commander-in-Chief were abolished. He
would not accept any lowering of his own status or
dignity.[2] The Queen said that Lord Wolseley and General
Buller were horrified at the report, holding the opinion
that it was impossible to carry out the recommendations.[3]
Lord Wolseley's own comment was that "we [the army]
sorely want a doctor, I admit, but Brackenbury & Co.
have sent us an executioner".[4]

[1] *Queen Victoria's Letters*, 1886–1901, I, pp. 582–4. [2] *Ibid.* p. 594.
[3] *Ibid.* p. 594. [4] *Ibid.* pp. 582–4.

Five years were to elapse before the sweeping recommendations of the Commission were to be adopted even in a modified form with a Commander-in-Chief superimposed, a variation of the scheme which its authors had not contemplated. Meanwhile, the report formed the basis of discussion in political and military circles, and it was generally felt that steps must be taken to carry out some reform of army administration. However, but small progress in that direction had been made by the time Lord Salisbury went out of office in 1892. Gladstone became Prime Minister for the fourth time in the August of that year, and appointed Campbell-Bannerman—"a good honest Scotchman" as Queen Victoria once called him—Secretary of State for War. He prepared a scheme which took definite shape in May, 1895, and although generally approved by the other members of the Cabinet, was not put into force until a later date on account of a change of government.

Under this plan, the Joint Naval and Military Council was not formed, but a Defence Committee of the Cabinet, which the professional advisers of both services could be invited to attend, was established. A War Office Council was set up. Its duties were apparently consultative, and not executive. It was presided over by the Secretary of State, with the Commander-in-Chief as first military member, while his military subordinates were of equal standing as members of the Council.[1] The office of Commander-in-Chief was retained, but the period of tenure of that office was strictly limited in future to five years. To the Queen, this proposed time-limit was a "deathblow to the cherished fiction that the Com-

[1] Spender, *Life of Campbell-Bannerman*, I, p. 146.

mander-in-Chief was the permanent personal deputy of the Sovereign ".[1]

It was proposed to make the Commander-in-Chief the Chairman of an Army Board, with the heads of the principal military departments as members.

The Board would select officers alike for promotion and for staff appointments, would make proposals for estimates, and deal with all questions referred to it by the Secretary of State; it would also form part of a War Office consultative Council in conjunction with the Under-Secretary of State, the Financial Secretary, and other specially nominated officers, the Council itself being under the direct control of the Secretary of State.[2]

The Commander-in-Chief was to issue orders to the army and be responsible for all decisions on military matters. At the same time, the heads of the different military departments at the War Office were to have the right of direct access to the Secretary of State, the idea being to give them more definite responsibility for the duties they were called upon to perform. This scheme of administrative reform appealed to the lay mind, but its weak point was that the authority of the Commander-in-Chief over the military departments for which he was to be held responsible, could be but nominal in reality if his subordinates could approach the Secretary of State without reference to him.

The Cabinet, over which Lord Rosebery now presided, was faced with a difficult question in regard to the next step to be taken in the policy they had adopted. In 1871, when the Duke of Cambridge had been in office for about

---

[1] Lee, *Life of Queen Victoria*, p. 512; Newton, *Life of Lord Lansdowne*, pp. 133-4.
[2] *Wolseley's Life*, p. 271; Spender, *Life of Campbell-Bannerman*, I, p. 146.

thirteen years, the question was raised whether a change in Commander-in-Chief might not be beneficial to the army. Cardwell, in introducing the estimates, stated that the government were of the opinion that his continuance in office and his removal must depend on considerations of public policy. A few days afterwards, a motion to the effect that no scheme of military organisation could be considered complete which did not alter the tenure of the Commander-in-Chief's appointment in such a way that the Secretary of State could avail himself of the best administrative talent and most recent military experience of the British army, was defeated in the House of Commons. Twenty-four years elapsed before the question of the removal of the Duke from the office of Commander-in-Chief was definitely raised, and it was to this question that the Cabinet had to address itself in 1895.

It was thought likely that, at the age of seventy-six, the Duke of Cambridge had no longer the energy to carry out, nor the wish to see, further alterations in the office of Commander-in-Chief which he had in fact, if not in title, held for about forty years. His conservatism in military matters, combined with the increasing burden of his age, made it improbable that he would agree to the scheme which the government desired to adopt. His biographer states that it was his intense loyalty to the throne, and his devotion to the army, which led him to believe in the advantages to the nation of having a member of the royal family of sufficient age and experience as Commander-in-Chief.[1] There is no doubt that both he and the Queen greatly disliked the changes which had been made in the army during the previous five-and-twenty years, but

[1] Verner, II, p. 393.

they feared, most of all, any attempt to disturb the existing status of the Commander-in-Chief and his relationship to the Crown. The Queen consistently deprecated anything which lessened the royal prerogative in relation to the army. Neither she nor the Duke of Cambridge realised how far the political parties were prepared to go in developing the theory that a Secretary of State must be as supreme in the War Office as he was in the Home Office, and that the Liberal party and, as she was soon to learn, their political opponents had come to the definite conclusion that personal feelings and traditions must be set aside if the army was to be placed upon a satisfactory basis. The problem of how best to secure the resignation of the Commander-in-Chief required delicate handling by the ministers, but the Duke of Cambridge came to their assistance by addressing a letter to the Queen on May 4th, 1895, in which he said he would not retire unless she desired him to do so. She replied on the 19th that, on the advice of her ministers, she had come to the conclusion that

considerable changes in the distribution of duties among the Headquarters of my Army are desirable. These alterations cannot be effected without reconstituting the particular duties assigned to the Commander-in-Chief, and, therefore, though with much pain, I have arrived at the decision that for your own sake as well as in the public interest, it is inexpedient that you should much longer retain that position, from which I think you should be relieved at the close of your autumn duties.[1]

On June 21st the Secretary of State announced the Commander-in-Chief's resignation, and stated that the functions and responsibilities of his office were to be

[1] Verner, II, pp. 395–6.

greatly modified.[1] The appointment of the new Commander-in-Chief, however, was to be in the hands of another government for, on the same afternoon, on a motion on the Army Estimates calling attention to the inadequacy of the supply of small-arm ammunition, Lord Rosebery's government found itself in a minority of seven in the House of Commons, and resigned office on the following day.

Thus ended the long reign of the Duke of Cambridge as Commander-in-Chief. The Prince Consort, supported by Baron Stockmar, had considered that his appointment would diminish the possibility of a revolution in this country. The Queen's idea was to confirm her personal attachment to the army by placing a member of the royal family at its head. She wished to assert her right to control it in face of the growing claims to supremacy, which were voiced with increasing strength in every Parliament and by every government. The Duke's opinion that great changes were unnecessary made progress in the direction of reform difficult.

Lord Lansdowne was the Secretary of State for War in Lord Salisbury's new administration, and one of his earliest duties was to obtain a Cabinet decision on future plans for War Office reform, in which a settlement of the vexed question of the appointment of a Commander-in-Chief to follow the Duke of Cambridge was a matter of paramount importance. Lord Rosebery had selected Sir Redvers Buller. The new government decided in favour of Lord Wolseley, who thus succeeded the "irremovable Royal Commander-in-Chief", with whom

[1] Vol. II of *Queen Victoria's Letters*, 1886–1901, contains many letters bearing on the Duke of Cambridge's resignation.

he had so often disagreed, and whose temper he had so often more than ruffled, in the highest position in the British army, although a proposal to appoint the Duke of Connaught now found favour with Queen Victoria as it did again in 1900 when Lord Wolseley retired.[1]

The next step was to consider the changes to be made in the War Office itself. The government practically adopted the whole of Campbell-Bannerman's plans, which, as has been shown above, were in fact a modified form of the recommendations of the Hartington Commission on the basis of a transfer of power from the military to the civil side. The new scheme was published in an Order-in-Council dated November 21st, 1895. The office of Commander-in-Chief with altered duties and responsibilities was maintained as a means of safeguarding the interests of the Crown in the army. The retention of the office of Commander-in-Chief was a radical alteration in the scheme drawn up by the Hartington Commission which, as has been seen, contemplated the direct responsibility of the heads of departments at the War Office to the Secretary of State. The government's decisions involved their simultaneous responsibility to both the parliamentary and the military heads of the office, an arrangement which was unsound from an administrative point of view.

Duties at the War Office were allocated as follows:

(1) The Commander-in-Chief was made the principal adviser of the Secretary of State on all military questions. He was to be responsible for the general command of the forces at home and abroad; for

---

[1] *Wolseley's Life*, pp. 275–6; Newton, *Life of Lord Lansdowne*, pp. 131, 133, 187; *Queen Victoria's Letters*, 1886–1901, II, p. 506, III, pp. 356, 592–5.

intelligence and mobilisation plans; for the general supervision of the military departments of the War Office; and for the appointments, promotions, and rewards of officers.

(2) The Adjutant-General was to be responsible for the discipline, training, recruiting and discharging of troops.

(3) The Quartermaster-General was to be responsible for food, forage, quarters, fuel, transport and pay.

(4) The Inspector-General of Fortifications was to be responsible for fortifications, barracks and engineer services.

(5) The Inspector-General of Ordnance was to be responsible for demands, inspections, and custody of warlike stores.

These officers formed a War Office Consultative Council over which the Secretary of State presided. The Commander-in-Chief was generally in charge of the four other branches, but all five were equally and directly responsible to the Secretary of State.

"The main principle of the change", said Mr Brodrick, the Under-Secretary of State of War, "is the separate responsibility of the military heads of the departments to the Secretary of State for their departments, and the focussing of military opinion by means of the Army Board presided over by the Commander-in-Chief."[1]

In effect, the centralisation of responsibility in the hands of the Commander-in-Chief which had been introduced in 1888 was abolished by this re-distribution of duties. He was placed in a fresh relationship to the Secretary of

[1] Gwynn and Tuckwell, *Life of Sir Charles Dilke*, II, p. 424.

State and the principal members of the military staff, occupying a position analogous to that of a Chief of Staff.[1]

It was an unfortunate compromise in that it made the Commander-in-Chief generally responsible for the military branches of the War Office without giving him full authority over the heads of those branches who were independent of him in their dealings with the Secretary of State. The Commander-in-Chief was in an anomalous position, as Lord Wolseley realised before he ended his five years' tenure of that high office. The scheme was not a success from a military point of view. Early in 1897 he recorded in his diary that he was the vice-chairman of a debating society, and that the Secretary of State was the Commander-in-Chief as far as there was one.[2] Later on, he wrote to the Duke of Cambridge that the system was "only a drag on our military coach". As his biographers state, Lord Wolseley had overlooked the political implications of the Order-in-Council of 1895.[3] He had been warned and consulted by Lord Lansdowne about the considerable changes that were to be made in the status and duties of the Commander-in-Chief, but he did not realise that the politicians were bent on securing a much greater measure of supremacy over the army for the Secretary of State in future than previous occupants of that office had ever enjoyed before. Lord Wolseley failed to gauge the determination of the government to further the control of the army by the Secretary of State as the representative of Parliament.

Before he retired from office in 1900, Lord Wolseley addressed a memorandum to Lord Salisbury, at the

[1] Sir Almeric Fitzroy, *Memoirs*, I, p. 47.
[2] *Wolseley's Life*, p. 293.   [3] *Ibid.* p. 291.

Queen's request, stating his objections to the Order-in-Council of November, 1895. It was afterwards published as a parliamentary paper.[1] He pointed out that the Commander-in-Chief had no effective control, while the heads of the departments were not fully responsible. He said that the office of Commander-in-Chief had a high-sounding title with no responsibility, and advocated that one man should control all training, command, and discipline. The Commander-in-Chief should be given real powers or his office abolished. Lord Lansdowne's view was that the supervision allowed gave the Commander-in-Chief the right of any intervention he required, and his position as chief adviser of the Secretary of State gave his office all the importance in which he (the Commander-in-Chief) thought it lacking. He considered that part of the difficulties in South Africa was largely due to the fact that the Commander-in-Chief had been only generally responsible.[2] In a debate in the House of Lords in March, 1901, Lord Wolseley, who was warmly supported by Lord Northbrook, reiterated his complaint that the Order-in-Council of 1895 had undermined the Commander-in-Chief's authority. It had made him practically powerless to effect anything in face of a system under which the principal members of the War Office Council were directly under the Secretary of State, whom he compared to a householder who should be guided by the opinion of the foreman of works instead of consulting the architect. In reply, Lord Lansdowne challenged the competence of the witness. He said that Lord Wolseley had preferred to efface himself or to be energetic spasmodically, which was more embarrassing than efface-

[1] 1901 (Cd. 512).   [2] *Ibid.* p. 5; cf. *Wolseley's Life*, pp. 295-9.

ment, and that on matters where he should have spoken with authority, he had furnished neither light nor leading.[1]

In the meantime, events connected with the war in South Africa had proved the need for some measure of administrative reform. In 1901, the Clinton Dawkins Committee brought forward a number of proposals.[2] The principle of decentralisation from an overburdened War Office was advocated and led to the appointment of local auditors in commands, and the attachment of finance branches to the different military departments at the War Office together with various other administrative changes. It also recommended the reconstitution of the War Office Council with the addition of the Director-General of Mobilisation and Military Intelligence and the Director-General of the Army Medical Services. By Order-in-Council of November 4th, 1901, the Adjutant-General, the Director-General of Mobilisation and Military Intelligence, and the Military Secretary were brought under the "control" of the Commander-in-Chief, while the Quartermaster-General, the Inspector-General of Fortifications, the Inspector-General of Ordnance, and the Director-General of the Army Medical Services were placed under his "supervision". The Commander-in-Chief remained the principal military adviser of the Secretary of State as well as the inspector-general of all the land forces. This re-arrangement was an admission of the justice of some of the criticisms levelled by Lord Wolseley against the system which had existed during his term of office. The War Office Council, set up to advise the Secretary of State, met from time to time at first, and

[1] Sir Almeric Fitzroy, *Memoirs*, I, p. 47.
[2] 1901, c. 581.

then weekly, under his chairmanship, to consider matters referred to it by him or which other members suggested. At the same time, an Army Board under the Commander-in-Chief discussed proposals for the estimates, questions of promotion in the higher ranks, and, during the South African War, details of mobilisation. The establishment of two consultative committees in the one department, presided over by two functionaries, whose respective spheres of duties had led to so much bitter antagonism in the past, was a retrograde step and suggested a possible reversion to the bygone days of squabbles and bickerings between Whitehall and Pall Mall.

The report of the Royal Commission on the War in South Africa, published in 1902, delivered a verdict which was favourable in some respects to the military administration, but declared that "the want of consultative power" was still a defect in War Office administration; that the various Committees and Boards within that office were too numerous and indeterminate in their functions; and that the War Office Council required definition as to its duty, and of permanence as to its character.[1] The general tenor of the report proved that the time had come once again for some serious measures of reform to be undertaken. King Edward VII pressed for drastic changes, wishing to do "everything possible to secure the efficiency of the troops who will in the event of war be first sent on active service".[2] The country as a whole was seriously alarmed by the disclosure of various defects in the machinery of army administration, and there was an unmistakable call for the whole system to be

[1] *Report of Commission on War in South Africa* (Cd. 1789), pp. 132–43.
[2] Lee, *Life of King Edward VII*, II, p. 193.

placed upon a definitely practicable basis of an enduring character.

Balfour succeeded his uncle, Lord Salisbury, as Prime Minister in 1902, and a determined effort was inaugurated to provide the country with a military organisation of a permanent and workable nature. It was not "tinkering" with the army as an army that was required, but a thorough revision of headquarters was necessary if the machine as a whole was to become efficient. Re-arrangements in army administration outside the War Office could follow. The urgent, essential problem was to see that the heart of the organisation was sound; that the machinery of the central office was placed on a more businesslike footing than before; and that the dangers of dual control by the Secretary of State and the Commander-in-Chief with its concomitants of jealousy and irritation were obliterated. The Commission on the South African War had recorded the pressing need of reform. As a step in the direction of carrying out its recommendations in this respect, a War Office Reconstitution Committee was appointed in 1903. Its chairman was Lord Esher. As a member of the Commission on the late war, he had written a memorandum as an appendix to its report, in which he had advocated the reorganisation of the War Office Council with internal decentralisation, and the abolition of the post of Commander-in-Chief. The other members of the Committee were Sir John, afterwards Lord, Fisher, and Sir George Clarke, afterwards Lord Sydenham.

The Esher Committee, as this body came to be called, was directed by its terms of reference to take the Admiralty system of higher administration as the basis of its

action. It issued a series of illuminating and interesting
reports, but no evidence to show the basis of its recommendations was published.[1] It pointed out that the War
Office had been administered from the point of view of
peace, and that it was considered necessary "to make a
complete break with the past, and to endeavour to re-
constitute the War Office with a single eye to the effective
training and preparation of the Military Forces of the
Crown for war". Attention was drawn to the frequent
changes, and lack of stability in administration, at the
War Office; to the numerous and scathing criticisms of
the department which had been passed by endless Committees and Commissions; to the lack of any organic reorganisation since the Crimean War; to the failure to do
anything after the Hartington Commission had made its
drastic proposals for reform. It went on to say:

The relations of the Secretary of State to the Military Heads
of the War Office are not such as to enable him to discharge
his duties to the best advantage. The centralisation of a vast
number of incongruous functions in the Commander-in-
Chief results in the neglect of work of primary importance.

At the same time, the duties and responsibilities of the
Military Heads are ill-defined, and their relations to each other
and the Secretary of State are not such as effective administration demands.

We consider that, as a first step in the reconstruction of the
War Office, the position of the Secretary of State should be
placed on precisely the same footing as that of the First Lord
of the Admiralty, and that all submissions to the Crown in
regard to military questions should be made by him alone.

It was recognised, both by the Hartington Commission and
by the members of the War Commission who signed the
minority report, that the high office of Commander-in-

[1] *Parl. Papers*, 1904 (Cd. 1932), (Cd. 1968) and (Cd. 2002).

Chief, as hitherto defined, is inconsistent with the principle of administration of the Army by the Secretary of State and a Board or Council.

We therefore consider that it is imperative to abolish the office of Commander-in-Chief, which was only revived as late as 1887, and we urge the divorce of administration from executive command and the decentralisation of the latter.[1]

The main recommendations of the Committee were: the establishment of an Army Council on similar lines to the Board of Admiralty but modified to meet the special conditions of the army; the abolition of the office of Commander-in-Chief; and the creation of a Chief of Staff. They "reiterated in a curt and dogmatic form" the proposals made by the Hartington Commission in 1890.[2] The Committee completed its work in 1904, and the Cabinet established an Army Council by Letters Patent and Order-in-Council dated February 6th of that year.

The Letters Patent appointed the Army Council "for the administration of matters pertaining to our Military Forces and the defence of Our Dominions". The Council was the centre of the whole scheme and, with the Secretary of State as chairman, was to consist of the following members who were each allotted certain specified duties:

(1) 1st Military Member—Chief of Staff—military policy generally.

(2) 2nd Military member—Adjutant-General—personnel and discipline.

(3) 3rd Military member—Quartermaster-General—supply.

[1] *Report*, Pt I, Sec. II, paras. 8–10, 18.
[2] Anson, *Law and Custom of the Constitution*, II, Pt II, p. 206.

(4) 4th Military member—Master-General of Ordnance—armaments and fortifications.

(5) Parliamentary Under-Secretary of State.

(6) Financial Secretary.

(7) Permanent Under-Secretary of State.

Under this settlement, the Secretary of State for War became as supreme in all phases of military administration as the First Lord of the Admiralty had been in naval questions for many years. Henceforward, the Secretary of State was to be the recognised channel of communication between the Sovereign and the army. He became the adviser of the Crown on all military matters and responsible for the exercise of the royal prerogative. He was given full powers to allocate duties to the members of the Army Council, of which the military members have been called "the nominees and instruments of the Secretary of State".[1] He occupied the logical position of being in full control of the department over which he was called to preside. He was answerable to Parliament, from that time onwards, for the discipline of the army, its relations to the civil populations, its cost and efficiency, in fact, for everything connected with it.

Until the Army Council was created, successive Secretaries of State were faced with an adviser in the shape of a Commander-in-Chief, overburdened with work, who was not in the closest touch with the actual daily work of the army; and was, perhaps, out of harmony with the aspirations of those in more direct contact with battalion

---

[1] Cf. the re-allocation of the respective duties of the Quartermaster-General and the Master-General of the Ordnance in 1927.

and regimental commanders. The new organisation
placed at the disposal of the Secretary of State a series of
military advisers, each of whom would be a soldier of
distinction and experience, and each of whom would be
individually responsible to the Secretary of State for his
department of the War Office.

With the promulgation of the government's decision
adopting the recommendations of the Esher Committee,
the struggle for supremacy between the civil and military
authorities came to an end. In its earlier phases, it had
taken the shape of an acute controversy between Parliament and the army itself, in which the armed forces had
not hesitated to use their power to coerce the constitutional institutions of the country. Parliament in its turn
abused the power it wielded as the controller of the public
purse. It feared or seemed to fear that the army might be
turned against itself, and claimed, as representing the
collective political wisdom of the nation, the right to
curtail or even abolish the army altogether. As time went
on, and the recollections of the failure of the Commonwealth to govern by military forces faded into the distance,
the passions aroused by the dispute became less heated.
Opinions became more balanced. Judgments were given
more dispassionately. Sound common-sense and political
intelligence gradually pointed the way to a solution of the
difficulties.

Meanwhile, the Crown occupied a special position in
relation to the army. By custom and practice, the
Sovereign had been recognised as the head of the army
and, in that capacity, had always maintained a close relationship with it. Any changes in the administration of
the army were closely and jealously watched, and any

proposals which might affect its connection with the Crown were studied with an attention suggesting that the army as an institution was the personal property of the Sovereign. This tendency was developed in a marked degree during Queen Victoria's long reign. It was at this juncture that the policy of enforcing the supremacy of the Secretary of State first became almost a catchword in discussions of military, administrative reform. The wish was common to the two political parties and, in the end, both took steps to achieve their object; the Liberals, with the partial amalgamation of the Horse Guards and the War Office during Cardwell's tenure of the office of Secretary of State for War; the Conservatives, with the establishment of the Army Council during Balfour's administration.

It is important to note that no attempt was made to interfere with the powers of the King as head of the army. The issue of whether the King could regulate the army as he pleased was not raised. To have done so, would have involved a discussion of the controversy which has centred round the question of the possession by the Sovereign of some power which cannot be abolished or controlled by Act of Parliament. The "prerogative", as this power is called, was defined by Professor Dicey as

the name for the residue of discretionary power left at any moment in the hands of the Crown, whether such power be in fact exercised by the King himself or by his Ministers. Every act which the executive Government can lawfully do without the authority of the Act of Parliament is done in virtue of this prerogative.[1]

When the Statute Law Revision Act of 1863 was passed,

---

[1] Dicey, *Laws of the Constitution*, pp. 61, 421.

it left unrepealed that part of the preamble of the Act of 1660 which stated that

within all his Majesties realmes and dominions the sole supreme government command and disposition of the Militia and of all forces by sea and land and of all forts and places of strength is and by the lawes of England ever was the undoubted right of His Majesty and his royall predecessors Kings and Queens of England and that both or either of the Houses of Parliament cannot nor ought to pretend to the same.[1]

This preamble, which is still in force to-day, gives authority to the statement which describes succinctly the present position that

the government of the forces is vested in the Crown, who has power to make regulations as to command and administration.[2]

The means by which the present settlement of this question was reached have been discussed in the foregoing pages. It was carried out by the same process of gradual and laborious development which has marked the growth of so great a part of the unwritten constitution of the country. Years of discussion and inquiry, seemingly fruitless, apparently superfluous, leading to nothing beyond a pile of dusty bluebooks and columns of print in Hansard and the daily press, were the means by which public opinion was educated to understand, appreciate, and permit the changes in army administration which were made in the end with such suddenness in 1904.

No doubt, the Army Council system can be criticised like all human institutions. Among other things, it has

[1] 13 Car. II, c. 6.
[2] Halsbury, *Laws of England*, xxv, p. 37, sec. 69.

been said that it retards business; that it does not suit our English organisation; that it is a failure.[1] In answer, it can be said that under the leadership of Lord Haldane, it made ready the army that went to France in 1914, better trained and better prepared in every way than any army sent across the seas to fight the country's battles at any earlier time in history.

The system stood the test of a great war and, even if there is no finality in such questions, some words written by Lord Wolseley may well be remembered by those who advocate further changes:

> Under a system of Parliamentary government like ours, it is no easy matter to devise a system that will at one and the same time maintain the Army upon purely military lines and under the sole command of soldiers, and will also give to the Secretary of State for War that general control over the Army, its numbers, and the expenditure of the money voted to it, which is essentially necessary under our Constitution.[2]

[1] Lord Grenfell, *Memoirs*, p. 148.
[2] *Wolseley's Life*, pp. 292–3.

EPILOGUE

ALTHOUGH the long struggle described in the preceding pages came to an end when the Army Council was established, it may not be out of place to touch upon certain subsequent developments connected with the control of the armed forces.

As has been seen, many of the schemes inaugurated during the Cardwell regime at the War Office were unfinished when he resigned the seals of office. It was left to others to build upon the foundations he had laid, and it took thirty-four years to give effect to many details of the policy he had initiated. These years witnessed the gradual creation of a bolder and less petty outlook on questions of national and imperial defence. The path of progress was stony, and many vicissitudes were encountered. Nevertheless, the advance, in spite of the humiliating episode of the war in South Africa, was made successfully, and a new outlook on military affairs characterised the opening years of the present century.

The weakness in military organisation which had been so ruthlessly exposed during that campaign led to the production of a series of proposals for army reform, but nothing had been carried into effect by the time that Balfour's government went out of office in 1905. The difficulties of the political situation abroad and at home were not without their influence on the development of our military plans. The salient features may be recalled in a few sentences. The international situation gradually assumed a threatening complexion. The so-called Peace Conference at the Hague in 1907 did little or nothing to alleviate the dangers with which the world was beset. Relations between France and Germany were seriously strained. Their acute differences of opinion in regard to Morocco gravely compromised the prospects of a continuance of peace. The development of friendly relations between England and France, which followed the establishment of the Entente Cordiale, together with the Franco-Russian alliance and the settlement of various outstanding difficulties between Great Britain and Russia, aroused feelings of jealousy and suspicion throughout Germany, where belief that that Empire was being encircled by a ring of hostile powers was sedulously fostered. The Balkan Wars alarmed the Chancelleries of the Great Powers by the lurking menace of repercussions far beyond South-Eastern Europe. An attack on this country by Germany was a matter of everyday discussion. The possibility of a hostile landing under the cover of the German fleet, which had rapidly increased since the first step in naval rivalry with Great Britain was taken by the passage of the Navy Bill through the Reichstag in 1900, was openly canvassed. Lord Roberts fathered the National Service campaign as a proposed method of increasing this country's means of self-defence. There was a vague feeling of uncertainty as to what Great Britain and Ireland would be called upon to do in the event of war between France and Germany. Comparatively few people knew about, or understood, what the guarantee of the maintenance of Belgium's independence involved, although it was recorded in all histories of modern Europe and had been discussed in Parliament at the time of the Franco-Prussian War. At home the country was passing through a period of embittered domestic political controversy, in which feelings ran high on such subjects as the Budget of 1909–10, the powers of the House of Lords, the Parliament Act and Home Rule.

The difficulties of a war minister in any democratically governed country during those fateful years were bound to be acute. They were augmented here by the national characteristic which prefers not to face the possible eventuality of war until fighting can no longer be avoided. In addition, the defects of a political system which places two or more parties in a position of rivalry have to be overcome. They have their pet panaceas for the country's ills and strive for place and power as the only means of testing the efficacy of their particular nostrums. The Cabinet of the day has to find the means of holding together its majority in the House of Commons, without which it cannot hope to remain in office and carry its financial estimates. Ministers had their difficulties about army votes in the eighteenth century and again, after Waterloo, when it was believed that the Congress of Vienna had settled all European international questions for all times. To-day, it is easier for ministers to gain approval for their financial proposals. Supporters of the government are less likely to go the length of voting against it on the estimates, as the carrying of a motion for their reduction involves the resignation of the government.

Nevertheless, a war minister who belongs to a party that is pledged to peace and retrenchment is bound to find great difficulties in his endeavours to obtain approval for his estimates. His own party accuses him of wasting money on armaments. His opponents argue that he is not spending enough. A third party advocates the allotment

162   PARLIAMENT AND THE ARMY

of larger amounts to the Navy or Air Force at the expense of the Army. If domestic politics proved to be a hindrance to a war minister who was anxious to put the organisation of the country's military forces on a sound footing, the trend of events in Europe made it only too clear that there was no time to waste if the nation was to be in a position to fulfil its obligations abroad when the seemingly inevitable call came to do so. It fell to the lot of Haldane as Secretary of State for War in Sir Henry Campbell-Bannerman's Cabinet, which came into office in 1905, to carry out the necessary reforms. When he took office, the army was not ready for war. There was no divisional organisation. There was hardly a brigade which could have been dispatched to Europe without some re-arrangement. The general principle adopted by Haldane and his advisers was to complete the Cardwell Scheme by organising the home-service battalions into six infantry divisions, complete with artillery, engineers, medical and other services, so that they could be dispatched to a theatre of war with the minimum loss of time. The complete series of reforms carried out between 1906 and 1912 may be summarised as follows:

(1) The formation of a General Staff under the Chief of Staff (later Chief of the Imperial General Staff) with three Directors for (a) Military Operations, (b) Staff Duties, and (c) Military Training.

(2) The establishment of an Expeditionary Force of 6 Divisions and 1 Cavalry Division—150,000 men.

(3) The "Militia" became the "Special Reserve" to supply drafts for the Regular Army in War.

(4) The Volunteers and Yeomanry organised as a Terri-

torial Force of 14 Divisions and 14 Cavalry Brigades organised on the same lines as the Regular Army. This arrangement provided for the expansion of the military forces for a big war. County Associations were made largely responsible for raising and administering this Force.

(5) An Officers' Training Corps was established as a means of providing for the training and supply of officers for the Territorial Force and Reserve of Officers and to furnish a supply of officers with some military training in case of a big war.

(6) Formation of a Supplementary Reserve of Officers.

(7) The Dominions were asked to co-operate.

In the meantime, the wider aspects of imperial defence were studied with the closest possible attention. After the conclusion of the war in South Africa, it was considered that the right moment had arrived for a close investigation of that problem. There were two main questions to be borne in mind in any consideration of the future of imperial defence. They were, firstly, the relationship between this country and the Dominions and Colonies with their armed forces, and, secondly, the position of the navy in relation to the armed forces of the Empire, a matter of the greatest importance as the Empire's wars were amphibious wars.

The machinery to be employed in the conduct of this investigation was already in existence in an embryonic form. A Colonial Defence Committee had been organised in 1885.[1] A few years later, the Hartington Com-

[1] Colonial Defence questions were considered by the Committee for Trade and Plantations appointed by William III, q.v. Thompson, *The Secretaries of State*, 1681–1782, pp. 43, 44, 70.

mission had advocated "the formation of a Naval and Military Council, which should probably be presided over by the Prime Minister, and consist of the Parliamentary heads of the two services, and their principal professional advisers". A Defence Committee of the Cabinet was established by Lord Salisbury's third government and was a step towards the future Committee of Imperial Defence, but its functions were never clearly defined. It had no secretariat, and kept no records. It was largely engaged in settling controversies between the Admiralty, the War Office, and the Treasury.[1]

In 1901 Balfour established the Committee of Imperial Defence, to which the old Committee of 1885 was subordinated in 1904. The new Committee was arranged on the widest possible basis so that the Dominions could be represented when matters of interest to them were to be discussed. It was provided with a secretariat, and considered strategical schemes affecting every aspect of imperial defence. It provided a centre where statesmen, sailors and soldiers could meet in council and investigate grave questions of high policy in a manner that had never been possible before.

The creation of an Imperial General Staff in 1909 was a matter of great importance.[2] Its objects were explained at the Imperial Conference in 1907, and the concurrence of the Dominions was secured. The main functions of this staff were to be the study of military science in all its branches; the preparation of defence schemes on a common basis; the collection and distribution of in-

[1] *Report of Royal Commission on War in South Africa*, 1903, p. 135.
[2] In 1909, the title of "Chief of the General Staff" was changed to "Chief of the Imperial General Staff".

formation and intelligence; and the tendering of advice on training, education, and war organisation of Dominion forces at the request of a Dominion. It was hoped that the Committee of Imperial Defence would be used as a medium for consultation on matters of common concern, and that each Dominion would create a section of the General Staff on the lines of the General Staff in this country. While a system of the fullest possible co-operation in regard to organisation, training and equipment was considered desirable, it was understood that each Dominion would retain complete control of its forces. How well the work was done, was amply proved when mobilisation was ordered in 1914. In 1926 matters were carried a stage further by the establishment of the Imperial Defence College, in which facilities were offered to the Dominions for the study of these problems.

These pages are not the place in which to record or discuss its history, but two changes brought out by the Great War may be noted. In the first place, the Dominions, Colonies and the Indian Empire sent their armies in unprecedented numbers to fight side by side with the home forces. It was in this manner that the seed so carefully sown in the years preceding 1914 came to harvest, and outlying portions of the Empire won for themselves foremost places among the nations of the world. Secondly, at home, the enormous expansion of the Army in addition to the requirements of the Navy, the Air Force, the Mercantile Marine, and essential industries at home, compelled the adoption by Parliament of a measure of conscription as a means of making good the wastage of man-power in the military forces. This step was a violent departure from the time-honoured custom of dependence on the voluntary system, and was only sanctioned when it was apparent that the other alternative was to let the armies in the field perish for lack of adequate reinforcements.

There was no argument on the question of parliamentary control of the army, but there were indications that the old controversy on the relations which should exist between a Commander-in-Chief in the field and the ministers at home was still alive. Marlborough and Wellington were both confronted with it. Napoleon Bonaparte is quoted by Bourienne as saying at the time of the Campaign in Italy in 1796,

I never set the least account upon the plans received from the Directory. There are upon the spot too many circumstances to modify such instructions. The movement of a single corps of the enemy's army will completely overturn an entire plan arranged thus by the chimney corner. None but an old woman would put faith in such gossip.[1]

That statement contains the extreme military view of the subject, and it is not without interest to contrast it with the opinions of the late Lord Salisbury. Writing to Queen Victoria, in April, 1900, he said:

Under our present constitution, the doctrine that the Cabinet have *no* control over a General in the field is not practicable. If they have no control, of course they have no responsibility. In the case, which is, of course, possible, that some grave evil were to result from the policy of the General, the Cabinet could not accept the responsibility of what had been done, or be under any obligation to defend him in Parliament; and in case Parliament took an adverse view, a

---

[1] Bourienne, *Memoirs*, I, p. 63, ed. Constable's Misc.

condition of great embarrassment would result. Of course, the Cabinet should not interpose without serious cause.[1]

It is not proposed to discuss this subject in these pages. It has led to much controversy in the past, and the debatable points are still open to further argument.[2]

Modern means of communication in the shape of trains, telegraph, telephones, aircraft and wireless have gradually, but naturally, changed the whole outlook of the world on international problems. It is no longer a question of days while a Foreign Office courier is posting across Europe with important dispatches for delivery to a harassed Secretary of State in Downing Street. It is a question of the few minutes, perhaps, taken in telephoning from Berlin to Vienna, or from Brussels to the Hague. The work upon which the peace of the world may depend is conducted with a publicity which would have outraged the ideas of Metternich and shocked the less tender susceptibilities of Bismarck.

These developments, which have brought the whole world into a more intimate contact than our forefathers could ever have imagined possible, have been aided by the advancement of education and the growth of the daily press. Questions which were once debated by a limited circle of people are now discussed, in some fashion, by the millions. Technical subjects such as the method of employing naval or military forces are a common topic of conversation in every family, where the views of this or that military correspondent are aired as if endowed with a special brand of infallibility. The interest taken in such questions as the increase or reduction of a fleet, the move-

[1] *Queen Victoria's Letters*, 1886–1901, III, pp. 525–6.
[2] *The Army Quarterly* for July, 1932, contains an article on the subject.

ment of troops, or the trials of an aeroplane of a new model, are all symptomatic of the altered conditions brought about by these modern changes. The result is that questions of imperial defence have ceased to be entirely military problems. To-day, they are matters of interest to every household in the country when any great international struggle, like the war of 1914–18, necessitates the calling of the whole population to arms or compelling them to serve the country's needs in some definite capacity. The last war brought home to all thinking persons how closely imperial defence affected them. It introduced a whole series of unprecedented measures. It entailed many restrictions on the normal liberties of the citizen. The hand of government touched every phase of domestic as well as public life. The consumption of food and light was regulated; the importation of certain articles forbidden; and the press subjected to a strict censorship. Fuel was rationed. Movements by train and ship were restricted.

Of developments on the military side, the rapid conquest of the air, which led to the creation of the Royal Air Force as a third arm, and the vitally important question of the use of toxic chemicals in war, closely concern the non-combatant as well as the military population of the world. Another example, which affects the civilian population, is the spread of mechanical transport in the army, a departure which foreshadows a great measure of interference with the normal civilian transportation services on the outbreak of war, because it will be necessary to impress large numbers of mechanical transport vehicles for military service.

The intensified application of scientific processes to the

art of war, the modern practice of whole nations being enrolled for military service, and the consequent interference with the habitual life of the civil population during a period of hostilities, have forced the consideration of these questions on to an entirely different plane from that occupied prior to 1914. They are at least partly responsible for the desire to see if it is not possible to treat the whole question of armaments from an international point of view. The idea is not new. For instance, the late Tsar of Russia appealed to the world at the end of last century to investigate the subject, and two international conferences were held in accordance with his wishes. For a variety of reasons, little or nothing was then accomplished, and it required the shattering struggle of 1914–18 to show how vast were the destructive forces let loose in a world-war.

So far as the British Empire is concerned, the resulting changes are revolutionary. The status of the Dominions has completely altered since 1914. At the Peace Conference in 1919, they were recognised as independent nations in the British Commonwealth of Nations. They now take their share as equals with all other nations in the proceedings of the League of Nations, where politico-strategical problems are investigated with the representatives of other countries, and not only with members of the Empire. They occupy the dual position of being simultaneously members of the League, and of the British Commonwealth.

The gravity of the discussions at Geneva with their twin objects of preventing the recurrence of war and of arresting the so-called "competition in armaments", is difficult to exaggerate from an imperial point of view. Article VIII of the Covenant of the League of Nations, which lays down that the Council shall formulate plans for the reduction of the armaments maintained by the members of the League, opens up large questions in regard to the future control of military forces. It is to be noted that the Governments concerned retain their right to accept or reject the proposals. Once acceptance has been given, the size of the forces cannot be exceeded until the question of revision is undertaken by the League after an interval of ten years has elapsed. Article XVI of the Covenant states that it shall be the duty of the Council of the League to recommend what effective military, naval or air force the Members of the League shall severally contribute to the armed forces to be used to protect the Covenants of the League against any member of the League who resorts to war. New complications and possibilities in the control of a nation's armed forces are opened up by this clause, but so far, the signatories of the Covenant have not been called upon to fulfil their obligations in this direction. What developments the future holds in store remain on the lap of the gods.

CHRONOLOGICAL TABLE OF
PRINCIPAL EVENTS

1628　Petition of Right contained protests against billeting and martial law.

1641–2　House of Commons pressed for control of militia and of fortified places.

1642–9　Civil war.

1648　"Remonstrance" by army against Parliament's negotiation with King Charles.

Pride's Purge.

1653　Long Parliament terminated on expulsion of members by soldiers.

1655　Appointment by Cromwell of Major-Generals to control local affairs.

1658　Death of Cromwell.

Army attempted to govern the country.

1660　The Restoration.

Beginning of the future standing army.

1661　Troops raised to garrison Tangiers.

1663　Reorganisation of militia.

1667　Clarendon impeached.

1679　Billeting declared illegal.

1688　Landing of the Prince of Orange at Torbay.

1689　The Revolution.

Declaration of Right stated that the keeping of a standing army by the King was illegal unless with the consent of Parliament.

First Mutiny Act passed.

Second Mutiny Act legalised billeting.

1690　Parliament voted money definitely for war against France and in Ireland. The beginning of modern system of appropriation.

1697　Peace of Ryswick followed by reduction of the army to ten thousand men by order of Parliament; further reductions in 1698.

1701　War of Spanish Succession. Increase in the strength of the army voted by Parliament.

1707　Union of England and Scotland. Military establishments united.

1713　Treaty of Utrecht. Reduction of the army.

1715　Rebellion in Scotland.

1745   Rebellion in Scotland. Army mostly abroad; militia unready.
1756–63   Seven Years' War. Army largely increased.
1757   Militia Act.
1775–83   War with American Colonies.
1783   Burke's Bill for Economical Reform defined responsibilities of Secretary-at-War as regards financial and civil business of the army.
1793   War with France.
          Lord Amherst appointed Commander-in-Chief.
          The Adjutant-General's and Quartermaster-General's Departments transferred to office of Commander-in-Chief from that of Secretary-at-War.
1794   Secretary of State for War appointed for first time.
1795   Duke of York appointed Commander-in-Chief.
1799   Duke of York advocated control of the whole military service, including finance, by the Commander-in-Chief. A compromise arranged which left finance with Secretary-at-War; the Commander-in-Chief to be responsible for discipline, movements, quarterings, etc.
1800   Union of Great Britain and Ireland. Military establishments united.
1801   Secretary of State for War became Secretary of State for War and the Colonies on taking over colonial business from the Home Department.
1805   Questions of discipline placed under the Commander-in-Chief.
1809   Sir D. Dundas appointed Commander-in-Chief on resignation of the Duke of York.
          Renewal of controversy on relations of Commander-in-Chief and Secretary-at-War.
1811   Duke of York re-appointed Commander-in-Chief.
1812   Minute of the Prince Regent in Council upholding the supremacy of Secretary-at-War in regard to control of financial questions.
1815   Battle of Waterloo.
          Reduction and neglect of the army during the following years.
          Militia laws in abeyance.
          Disappearance of volunteers.
1827   Duke of Wellington appointed Commander-in-Chief on death of the Duke of York. He was succeeded by Lord Hill.
1829   Establishment of Metropolitan Police.
          The Irish Constabulary and County and Borough Police were established in 1836 and 1856 respectively.

1832   Consolidation of the Board of Admiralty.

1833   Commission of enquiry under the Duke of Richmond recommended the amalgamation of various military offices under a civilian minister; the Master-General of the Ordnance to be under the Commander-in-Chief.

1837   Lord Howick's Commission advocated the centralisation of the civil business of the army and the preparation of one estimate to cover all military expenditure.

1842   Duke of Wellington appointed Commander-in-Chief on resignation of Lord Hill.

1847   Duke of Wellington's letter to Sir J. Burgoyne on the military situation of the country.

1852   Militia reorganised.
Death of the Duke of Wellington.
Lord Hardinge appointed Commander-in-Chief.

1854–6   Crimean War. No reserves beyond ten thousand pensioners and twenty-five thousand to thirty thousand militia, who were not allowed to transfer. Weakness of military administration.
Secretary of State for War appointed to take over the military duties of the Secretary of State for War and the Colonies.
Board of Ordnance abolished, and its duties divided between the Secretary of State for War and the Commander-in-Chief.
Militia and Yeomanry transferred to the control of the War Department.
Commissariat transferred from the Treasury to the War Department.
Issue of supplementary patent to the Secretary of State with special reservation of powers of discipline, command, etc., to the Commander-in-Chief.

1856   Duke of Cambridge appointed General Officer Commanding on retirement of Lord Hardinge.

1857   "The War Department" became "the War Office".

1857–8   Reduction in the strength of the Army.

1860   Sir James Graham's Committee on Military Organisation recommended that the Horse Guards and War Office should be under the same roof.

1861   Sir G. Cornewall Lewis' memorandum on duties of Commander-in-Chief.

1862   House of Commons resolution in favour of self-governing colonies undertaking their own defence.

1863   Office of Secretary-at-War abolished.

1864–6   Prussian military successes aroused interest in military matters.

1866   Lord Strathnairn's Committee on transport duties of army in the field. "Department of Control" proposed.

1868-74 Cardwell Secretary of State for War.

1870   Horse Guards placed under one roof with the War Office, which was organised in three departments:
(1) Military—under Commander-in-Chief.
(2) Supply—under Surveyor-General.
(3) Finance—under Financial Secretary.
Army Enlistment Act introduced short service (total, 12 years: part with colours; part with reserve).
Colonial garrisons reduced so as to increase number of units at home, thus equalising the number of battalions at home and abroad.
Franco-Prussian War.

1871   Abolition of promotion by purchase.

1872   Militia placed under Commander-in-Chief instead of lords-lieutenant.
Regular battalions linked in pairs.
Government empowered to take over railways in a national emergency.

1875   Control Department abolished. The Commissariat, Ordnance and Pay Departments outside the War Office placed under the Commander-in-Chief.

1881   Linked battalions lost their numbers and given territorial titles.

1882   Egyptian War. Short Service army with reserves employed for first time.

1883   Commissariat followed by Ordnance and Pay departments placed entirely under the Commander-in-Chief.

1885   Colonial Defence Committee organised.

1887   Duke of Cambridge appointed Commander-in-Chief.
Weakness of military forces.
Abolition of Surveyor-General's office.
Commander-in-Chief made responsible for clothing, feeding, equipment and pay in addition to other military duties.

1888   War Office business divided between (1) military and (2) civil division, both under the Secretary of State.

1889   Hartington Commission appointed. Its main recommendations were:
(1) Establishment of a Joint Naval and Military Council.
(2) Abolition of appointment of Commander-in-Chief.
(3) Appointment of General Officer Commanding in Great Britain.

        (4) Appointment of Chief of Staff.

        (5) Establishment of permanent War Office Council.

1895   Resignation of Duke of Cambridge.

        Lord Wolseley appointed Commander-in-Chief.

        Alteration in duties and responsibilities of the Commander-in-Chief.

1899–1902 War in South Africa.

1901   Resignation of Lord Wolseley.

        Lord Roberts appointed Commander-in-Chief.

        Clinton-Dawkins Committee recommended decentralisation at the War Office.

        Committee of Imperial Defence established.

1903   Royal Commission on War in South Africa.

1904   Esher Committee's Report. Its principal recommendations were:

        (1) Establishment of an Army Council.

        (2) Abolition of the post of Commander-in-Chief.

        (3) Appointment of a Chief of Staff.

1905–12 Haldane Secretary of State for War.

1909   Creation of Imperial General Staff.

1914–18 The Great War.

1919   Peace Conference at Versailles.

        Establishment of the League of Nations.

1926   Imperial Defence College established.

NOTES ON AUTHORITIES CONSULTED

A LIST of some of the authorities consulted is appended. It is arranged alphabetically, under authors' and editor's names, and includes the titles of certain parliamentary papers. They relate to a selection of the reports of the numerous official Committees on military organisation which have reviewed the work of the War Office from time to time. I have purposely omitted the names of various memoirs such as those of Walpole, Hervey, Cornwallis, Greville, Croker, etc., to which students of the periods in which they were written must refer, if they wish to find out details of the contemporary, social and political gossip.

Anson, Sir W., *Law and Custom of the Constitution.*
Arthur, Sir G., *Life of Kitchener.*
Ashley, E., *Life of Lord Palmerston.*
Atlay, J. B., *Life of Lord Haliburton.*

Bacon, Admiral Sir R., *Life of Lord Fisher.*
Ballard, Brigadier-General C. R., *The Great Earl of Peterborough.*
Biddulph, General Sir R., *Lord Cardwell at the War Office.*

Charteris, Sir E., *William Augustus, Duke of Cumberland.*
Childers, Lieut.-Colonel S., *Life of the Rt Hon. Hugh C. E. Childers.*
Churchill, W. S., *Life of Lord Randolph Churchill.*
Clarendon, Earl of, *History of the Rebellion in England.*
Clode, C. M., *Military Forces of the Crown.*
Constitutionalist, *Army Administration in Three Centuries.*
Corbett, Sir J. S., *Monk.* (English Men of Action Series.)
Corbett, Sir J. S., *England in the Mediterranean.*

Delavoye, Capt. A. M., *Life of Lord Lynedoch.*
Douglas, Sir G. and Dalhousie, Sir G., *The Panmure Papers.*

Ellesmere, Earl of, *Personal Reminiscences of the Duke of Wellington.*

Firth, Sir C. H., *Oliver Cromwell.*
Fortescue, Sir J., *History of the British Army.*
Fortescue, Sir J., *Wellington.*
Furber, H., *Henry Dundas, 1st Viscount Melville.*

Gathorne-Hardy, A. E., *Gathorne-Hardy, 1st Earl of Cranbrook.*
Gibbs, Sir P., *Romance of George Villiers, Duke of Buckingham.*
Green, J. R., *Short History of the English People.*
Grenfell, Lord, *Memoirs.*
Guedalla, P., *Palmerston.*
Guizot, F., *Memoirs of George Monk, Duke of Albemarle.*
Gwynn, S. L. and Tuckwell, G. M., *Life of Sir Charles Dilke.*

Haldane, Viscount, *An Autobiography.*
Hannay, D., *Short History of the Royal Navy.*
Hardinge, Viscount, *Viscount Hardinge.* (Rulers of India Series.)
Holland, B., *Life of Duke of Devonshire.*
Hunt, W. and Poole, R. (edited by), *Political History of England from* B.C.
55 *to* A.D. 1901.

Ilbert, Sir C., *Parliament.*

Lecky, W. E. H., *History of England in the eighteenth Century.*
Lee, Sir S., *Life of Edward VII.*
Lee, Sir S., *Life of Queen Victoria.*

Macaulay, Lord, *History of England.*
Maitland, F. W., *Constitutional History of England.*
Mallet, B., *Life of Lord Northbrook.*
Martin, Sir T., *Life of the Prince Consort.*
Maurice, Sir F. and Arthur, Sir G., *Life of Lord Wolseley.*
Maxwell, Sir H., *Life of Wellington.*
Maxwell, Sir H., *Life of Rt Hon. W. H. Smith.*
Melville, Colonel C. H., *Life of General Sir Redvers Buller.*
Monypenny, W. F. and Buckle, G. E., *Life of Lord Beaconsfield.*
Morley, J., *Life of Richard Cobden.*
Morley, J., *Life of Gladstone.*

Namier, L. B., *Structure of Politics in the eighteenth Century.*
Namier, L. B., *England in the Age of the American Revolution.*
Newton, Lord, *Life of Lord Lansdowne.*

Official Reports:
  Reports of Commissions of Military Enquiry into Military Departments, 1806–12.
  Report of Select Committee on Army and Navy Appointments, 1833.
  Report on Consolidating the different departments of the Army, 1837.
  Report on Army and Ordnance Expenditure, 1849–50.
  Report on Civil and Professional Administration of the Naval and Military Departments, 1890.
  Report of the Royal Commission on the War in South Africa, 1903.
  Report of the War Office (Reconstitution) Committee, 1904.
Oliver, F. S., The Endless Adventure.

Parker, Sir C. S., Life of Sir James Graham.
Parker, Sir C. S., Life of Sir Robert Peel.

Queen Victoria's Letters, 1837–1901.

Rose, J. Holland, William Pitt and the Great War.
Rosebery, Earl of, Pitt. (Twelve English Statesmen Series.)

Sebag-Montefiore, C., A History of the Volunteer Forces from the earliest times to 1861.
Sheppard, Capt. E. W., A Short History of the Army to 1914.
Smith, G. C. Moore, Life of Field-Marshal Lord Seaton.
Spender, J. A., Life of Sir H. Campbell-Bannerman.
Stanhope, Earl, Notes of Conversations with the Duke of Wellington.
Stanmore, Lord, Memoirs of Sydney Herbert.

Thomson, M. A., The Secretaries of State, 1681–1782.
Thursfield, Sir J. R., Peel. (Twelve English Statesmen Series.)
Traill, H. D., William III. (Twelve English Statesmen Series.)
Trevelyan, G. M., England under Queen Anne—Blenheim.
Trevelyan, G. O., Life of Lord Macaulay.

Verner, Colonel W., Military Life of H.R.H. George, Duke of Cambridge.

Walton, Colonel C., History of British Standing Army, 1660–1700.
Wellington, Duke of, Speeches in Parliament.
Whitelock, B., Memorials of the English Affairs.
Wrottesley, Major-General G., Life and Correspondence of Field-Marshal Sir John Burgoyne.

Yorke, P. C., Life of Lord Chancellor Hardwicke.

INDEX

mission on position of, 135–7; in Campbell-Bannerman's scheme, 140–1; in Lansdowne's scheme, 145–7; Esher Committee on position of, 152–4; and members of the Army Council, 154; supremacy of, 154–5

Select Committee of 1860, *see* Military Organisation

Shippen, Sir William, speech by, against the army, 42

Short service, introduction of, 119; success of, in 1882, 130

Somers, Lord, and the Declaration of Right, 26; publishes his "Balancing Letter", 40

South Africa, Royal Commission on war in, report of, 150

Standing armies, English dislike of, 3–5; Clarendon and, 19; proposal for, in Scotland, 20; Earl of Peterborough's protest against, 23; Declaration of Right and, 26–7; first Mutiny Act and, 27–30; Parliament and, 33–5; pamphlets on, 39–40; Sir W. Shippen's speech on, 42; Dean Swift on, 42–3; opposition to, 44–5; effect of settlement of 1689 on, 57–9

Stephen Commission on army administration, 134

Strathnairn, Lord, and Committee on army transport, 115

Swift, Dean, on the army, 42–3

Tangiers, garrison for, and abandonment of, 17

Tarleton, Colonel, and enlistment of French Royalists, 51

Territorial Force, relations of, to Lords-Lieutenant, 124; creation of, 162–3

Test Act, the, and military commissions, 21; protest by Parliament on employment of officers

not complying with, 22; repeal of, supported by James II, 23

Tories, attitude of, to the army, 35, 41

Trained bands, command of, 7

Transport, control of, by Treasury, 73; Lord Strathnairn's Committee on, 115; under the Commander-in-Chief, 116

Treasury, the, control of supply and transport by, 73

Under-Secretary of State for War, the Permanent, as accounting officer, 33

United Services Club, the, foundation of, opposed, 54–5

Utrecht, the Treaty of, and reduction of army, 41

Volunteers, shortage of guns for, 134; as part of the Territorial Army, 162–3

War Department, *see* War Office

War Office, the, relations of, with Horse Guards, 97, 111–2; Northbrook Committee's recommendations as to the organisation of, 111–2; War Department becomes the, 111; divided into three departments, 113–4; allocation of duties at, in 1895, 145–6; under Esher Committee's report, 152–3; under Army Council scheme of 1904, 153–4 and *n*.

War Office Act of 1870, the, and the Secretary of State, 114

War Office Council, a, proposed by the Hartington Commission, 136–8; establishment of, 140, 146; proposed reconstitution of, 149–50; Royal Commission's remarks on, 150; Lord Esher on, 151

PRINTED BY WALTER LEWIS, M.A., AT THE UNIVERSITY PRESS, CAMBRIDGE

For EU product safety concerns, contact us at Calle de José Abascal, 56–1°, 28003 Madrid, Spain or eugpsr@cambridge.org.

www.ingramcontent.com/pod-product-compliance
Ingram Content Group UK Ltd.
Pitfield, Milton Keynes, MK11 3LW, UK
UKHW012345130625
459647UK00009B/545